The Royal Court Theatre presents
The Abbey Theatre production of

Portia Coughlan

by Marina Carr

Commissioned by the National Maternity Hospital, Dublin.

faber and faber
LONDON · BOSTON

First performed at the Royal Court Theatre on 9 May 1996.
First performed at the Peacock Theatre 21 March 1996.

The Royal Court Theatre is financially assisted by the
Royal Borough of Kensington and Chelsea.
Recipient of a grant from the Theatre Restoration Fund
& from the Foundation for Sport & the Arts.
The Royal Court's Play Development Programme is
funded by the Audrey Skirball-Kenis Theatre.
The Royal Court Registered Charity number 231242

National Maternity Hospital Dublin

the

commission

As part of its Centenary Celebrations the National Maternity Hospital commissioned Marina Carr to write a play. Portia Coughlan is the result and has been an outstanding success. Marina was based at the hospital while writing the play. The funding basis for the project was unique, coming exclusively from Irish women both at home and abroad. The National Maternity Hospital is both proud and delighted that the association, in this unique project, between Marina and the hospital has been so productive.

**Peter Boylan
Master**

Sponsors of the National Maternity Hospital centenary play

Margaret Behan
Joan Bergin
Maeve Binchy
Siobhan Bourke
Frances Boylan
Jane Brennan
Val Bresnihan
Joan Burton TD
Ann Butler
Fiona Coady
Helen Collins
Diana Connolly
Kitty Conroy
Sally Cooke
Barbara Cotter
Sinead Cotter
Ingrid Craigie
Una Crowley
Noelle Ann Curran
Jane Daly
Eunice D'Arcy
Ann Davy
Ruth Deeney
Anne Devitt
Veronica Donoghue
Geraldine Duffy
Edwina Dunn
Maeve Dwyer
Mary Ensor
Marie Fahy
Anne Fanagan
Margaret Fanagan
Maelbaine Fennelly
Alice Finlay
Maura Foley
Olwen Fouere
Brenda Fricker
Avril Gallagher
Mary Gallagher
Pauline Gibney
Bernice Godfrey
Freda Gorman
Roisin Grimley
The Linen Guild

Edel Hargaden
Teri Hayden
Sheila Healy
Carmencita Hederman
Jacinta Hogan
Garry Hynes
Anne Kelly
Helen Kilgallen
Anne King
Paula Ledbetter
Emily Lenehan
Aine Lynch
Geraldine Lynch
Laura MacDermott
Pamela M.Madigan
Katriona Maguire
Peggy Maguire
Maureen McGlynn
Moya McHugh
Esther Moriarty
Mary Murphy
Rose Mary O'Brien
Ann Rosemary O Callaghan
Eithne O Callaghan
Robina O'Driscoll
Marian O'Dwyer
Jacinta O'Herlihy
Oonagh O'Riordan
Harriet O'Donovan Sheehy
Aisling O'Sullivan
Niamh O'Sullivan
Marie Ostinelli
Lynne Parker
Deirdre Pepper
Sheila Pratschke
Sorcha Quigley
Fiona Shaw
Brigid Sheehy
Cathy Shubotham
Bernie Spillane
Miriam Stanley
Stephanie Stronge
Aine Sullivan
Irene Sullivan
Miriam Wiley

The Abbey Theatre Dublin

The Abbey Theatre is one of Ireland's most loved institutions. Founded by Yeats and Lady Gregory as a literary theatre dedicated to the production of Irish plays, it has enjoyed 90 years of success as our premier theatre. The years that followed the founding of the Abbey were a time of social and political upheaval in Ireland and this was occasionally reflected at the theatre. In 1907 there were riots when the first production of *The Playboy of the Western World* was staged. Undaunted the Abbey players went to the United States on tour establishing a precedent which has created a world-wide reputation for the theatre.

The Abbey was becoming recognised as a cultural asset and in 1925 the Government of the Irish Free State made provision for its National Theatre to be granted an annual grant, at a time when absolutely no other theatre in Britain, America or any part of the English-speaking world enjoyed such state assistance. But in 1926 the theatre-going audience once again revolted when O'Casey's first production of *The Plough and the Stars* was staged. The Abbey was developing something of a reputation for riotous behaviour!

In the years that followed the death of Lady Gregory (1932) the Abbey went from strength to strength, plays were now being produced in Irish and legendary figures such as Hugh Hunt, W. B. Yeats and Ernest Blythe were actively promoting theatre.

In 1951 the Abbey was destroyed by fire and the company moved to The Queens Theatre during a long period of rebuilding, because the foundation stone of the New Abbey was only laid by President De Valera in 1962. In 1966 the Abbey opened. A manager and artistic director were appointed to run the theatre.

By 1970 Brendan Behan's *Borstal Boy* had won a Tony Award on Broadway but back home another riot occurred during *A State of Chassis*. The early 70s saw the Abbey develop with artistic directors like Lelia Doolan (now director of the Irish Film Board) Thomas MacAnna and later Joe Dowling, Christopher Fitz-simon and Garry Hynes were to affirm the aspirations of its founders as the Abbey won one international award after another. These included the Olivier Award for *Hedda Gabler* and *Observe the Sons of Ulster Marching Towards the Somme,* the Edinburgh Fringe Award for *Mother of All the Behans* and *The Great Hunger*.

In 1990 Patrick Mason's production of *Dancing at Lughnasa* swept the boards in London and on Broadway. It was awarded a host of citations including the Olivier Award, the London Writers' Guild Best Play, The Tony Award for Best Play, Best Director and Best Featured Actress (New York). It also won the Outer Critics Circle Best Play, Best Director Award, the Drama Desk Best Ensemble, Best Director, the New York Drama Critics Best Play, the Theatre World Special Award and The Boree Log Award in Australia.

1994 saw J.M Synge's *Well of the Saints* take the Critics Circle Award at the Edinburgh Theatre Festival once again under the direction of Patrick Mason. The Abbey has continued its touring both nationally and internationally. The company toured to Moscow, Australia and the US and within Europe to France, Finland, Italy, Belgium and Greece. In 1996 it will attend the Imaginaire Irlandaise Festival in Paris touring from there to Copenhagen, Bonn and Brussels.

The Abbey Theatre remains Ireland's foremost cultural ambassador.

The Abbey Theatre
26 Lower Abbey Street
Dublin 1
Ireland

Telephone 00 353 1 8748741
Fax 00 353 1 872 9117

The English Stage Company at The Royal Court Theatre

The English Stage Company was formed to bring serious writing back to the stage. The Court's first Artistic Director, George Devine, wanted to create a vital and popular theatre. He encouraged new writing that explored subjects drawn from contemporary life as well as pursuing European plays and forgotten classics. When John Osborne's **Look Back in Anger** was first produced in 1956, it forced British Theatre into the modern age. But, the Court was much more than a home for *'Angry Young Men'* illustrated by a repertoire that ranged from Brecht to Ionesco, by way of J P Sartre, Marguerite Duras, Wedekind and Beckett.

The ambition was to discover new work which was challenging, innovative and also of the highest quality, underpinned by the desire to discover a truly contemporary style of presentation. Early Court writers included Arnold Wesker, John Arden, David Storey, Ann Jellicoe, N F Simpson and Edward Bond. They were followed by a generation of writers led by David Hare and Howard Brenton, and in more recent years, celebrated house writers have included Caryl Churchill, Timberlake Wertenbaker, Robert Holman and Jim Cartwright. Many of their plays are now regarded as modern classics.

Since 1994 the Theatre Upstairs has programmed a major season of plays by writers new to the Royal Court, many of them first plays, produced in association with the *Royal National Theatre Studio* with sponsorship from *The Jerwood Foundation*. The writers included Joe Penhall, Nick Grosso, Judy Upton, Sarah Kane, Michael Wynne, Judith Johnson, James Stock and Simon Block.

Many established playwrights had their early plays produced in the Theatre Upstairs including Anne Devlin, Andrea Dunbar, Sarah Daniels, Jim Cartwright, Clare McIntyre, Winsome Pinnock, and more recently Martin Crimp and Phyllis Nagy.

Theatre Upstairs productions have regularly transferred to the Theatre Downstairs, as with Ariel Dorfman's **Death and the Maiden**, and last autumn Sebastian Barry's **The Steward of Christendom**, a co-production with *Out of Joint*.

1992-1995 have been record-breaking years at the box-office with capacity houses for productions of **Faith Healer**, **Death and the Maiden**, **Six Degrees of Separation**, **King Lear**, **Oleanna**, **Hysteria**, **Cavalcaders**, **The Kitchen**, **The Queen & I**, **The Libertine**, **Simpatico**, **Mojo** and **The Steward of Christendom**.

Death and the Maiden and **Six Degrees of Separation** won the Olivier Award for Best Play in 1992 and 1993 respectively. **Hysteria** won the 1994 Olivier Award for Best Comedy, and also the Writers' Guild Award for Best West End Play. **My Night with Reg** won the 1994 Writers' Guild Award for Best Fringe Play, the Evening Standard Award for Best Comedy, and Best Comedy 1994 Olivier Awards. Jonathan Harvey won the 1994 Evening Standard Drama Award for Most Promising Playwright, for **Babies**. Sebastian Barry won the 1995 Writers' Guild Award for Best Fringe Play for **The Steward of Christendom**, Jez Butterworth was named New Writer of the Year for **Mojo** by the Writers' Guild, won the Evening Standard Award for Most Promising Newcomer 1995 and the 1996 Olivier Award for Best Comedy. Phyllis Nagy won the 1995 Writers' Guild Award for Best Regional Play for **Disappeared**. The Royal Court was the overall winner of the 1995 Prudential Award for the Arts for creativity, excellence, innovation and accessibility, and the 1995 Peter Brook Empty Space Award for innovation and excellence in theatre.

Donal McCann in Sebastian Barry's **The Steward of Christendom**

Photo: John Haynes

After nearly four decades, the Royal Court's aims remain consistent with those established by George Devine. The Royal Court Theatre is still a major focus in the country for the production of new work. Scores of plays first seen in Sloane Square are now part of the national and international dramatic repertoire.

How the Royal Court is brought to you

The English Stage Company at the Royal Court Theatre is supported financially by a wide range of public bodies and private companies, as well as its own trading activities. The theatre receives its principal funding from the **Arts Council of England**, which has supported the Royal Court since 1956. The **Royal Borough of Kensington & Chelsea** gives an annual grant to the Royal Court Young People's Theatre and provides some of its staff. The **London Boroughs Grants Committee** contributes to the cost of productions in the Theatre Upstairs.

Other parts of the Royal Court's activities are made possible by business sponsorships. Several of these sponsors have made a long-term commitment. 1996 will see the sixth Barclays New Stages Festival of Independent Theatre, supported throughout by **Barclays Bank**. **British Gas North Thames** supported three years of the Royal Court's Education Programme. Sponsorship by **WH Smith** helped to make the launch of the Friends of the Royal Court scheme so successful.

1993 saw the start of our association with the **Audrey Skirball-Kenis Theatre**, of Los Angeles. The Audrey Skirball-Kenis Theatre is funding a Playwrights Programme at the Royal Court. Exchange visits for writers between Britain and the USA complement the greatly increased programme of readings and workshops which have fortified the Royal Court's capability to develop new plays.

In 1988 the Royal Court launched the **Olivier Building Appeal** to raise funds to begin the task of restoring, repairing and improving the theatre building, made possible by a large number of generous supporters and significant contributions from the **Theatres Restoration Fund**, the **Rayne Foundation**, the **Foundation for Sport and the Arts** and the **Arts Councils Incentive Funding Scheme**.

The Royal Court earns the rest of the money it needs to operate from the Box Office, from other trading and from the transfers of plays such as **Death and the Maiden**, **Six Degrees of Separation**, **Oleanna** and **My Night With Reg** to the West End. But without public subsidy it would close immediately and its unique place in British Theatre would be lost. If you care about the future of arts in this country, please write to your MP and say so.

Portia Coughlan

by Marina Carr

Cast
in order of appearance

Portia Coughlan	**Derbhle Crotty**
Raphael Coughlan	**Sean Rocks**
Maggie May Doorley	**Marion O'Dwyer**
Senchil Doorley	**Des Keogh**
Damus Halion	**Don Wycherley**
Stacia, the Cyclops of Coolinarney	**Bronagh Gallagher**
Fintan Goolan	**Charlie Bonner**
Marianne Scully	**Stella McCusker**
Blaize Scully	**Pauline Flanagan**
Sly Scully	**Tom Hickey**
Gabriel Scully	**Peter Charlesworth Kelly**

Director	Garry Hynes
Designer	Kandis Cook
Lighting Designer	Jim Simmons
Music	Paddy Cunneen
Sound Designer	Dave Nolan
Assistant to the Designer	Patricia Mulligan
Stage Manager (London)	Martin Christopher
Deputy Stage Manager (London)	Debbie Green
Assistant Stage Manager (London)	Katy Hastings
Stage Manager (Dublin)	Colette Morris
Assistant Stage Manager (Dublin)	Susie Sheil
Voice Coach	Andrea Ainsworth
Set	Abbey Theatre Workshop
Costumes	Abbey Theatre Wardrobe
Make-up	Patsy Giles
Production Photographer (Ireland)	Amelia Stein
Production Photographer (London)	Ivan Kyncl

Marina Carr (writer)
Plays include: Low in the Dark, The Deer's Surrender, This Love Thing, The Mai, Ullaloo. She has received two bursaries in literature from the Arts Council. In 1994 she received a Henessy Award for her short story *Grow A Mermaid*. Marina is currently Ansbacher Writer-in Association at the Abbey Theatre.

Charlie Bonner
Theatre includes: The Cuchulainn Cycle (Trinity Players); London Assurance (Gate Theatre, Dublin), Volunteers (Lyric, Belfast); Wild Harvest (Barnstorm Theatre Company); Philadelphia, Here I Come!, Macbeth (Abbey Theatre, Dublin); Good Evening, Mr Collins, Monkey (Peacock Theatre, Dublin).
Radio includes: A Spot of Distress, Ballylenon.

Peter Charlesworth Kelly
Peter has been singing since he was eight. He was a chorister with the Palestrina Choir where he won the Junior Voice of the Future 1994. In December 1995 he sang the title role in Amahl and the Night Visitors with the RTE.

Kandis Cook (designer)
For the Royal Court: Pale Horse, Faith Healer, Women Beware Women, The Grace of Mary Traverse.
Design for theatre includes: Henry V, The Last Days of Don Juan, Epiceone, Bite of the Night, Arden of Faversham (RSC); Richard II, Love's Labours Lost

(Manchester Royal Exchange); Hamlet (Donmar Warehouse & Piccadilly); The Relapse (Lyric Hammersmith) Berenice, Dr Faustus, Britannicus.
Opera includes: Orpheus in the Underworld (ENO);Orlando (Wexford Festival).

Derbhle Crotty
Theatre includes: Gaslight (Druid Theatre Company); Measure for Measure (Gallowglass tour); Sandra/Manon (Dublin Theatre Festival); Katie Roche, The Mai (Peacock Theatre, Dublin); The Well of Saints (Abbey, Edinburgh Festival, Perth Festival); Miss Julie (Vesuvius Arts Company); Playing the Wife (Richmond, Guilford, Chichester).
Television includes: Gold in the Streets, Poorhouse.

Paddy Cunneen (music)
Paddy Cunneen has worked extensively as a composer and music director in theatre companies throughout the UK and Ireland. He is an associate director of Cheek by Jowl and has written music for all of their productions since 1988.

Pauline Flanagan
Theatre includes: Medea, Corpse, Steaming, The Innocents, Under Milkwood, Step on a Crack, The Father, The Complaisant Lover, The Living Room, God and Kate Murphy (Broadway); Celebration, Close of Play, Ulysses in Nightown, Drums Under the Window, Yeats, A Celebration!, Grandchild of the Kings

(nomination for New York Outer Critics Circle Award), Philadelphia Here I Come! (Off-Broadway); Juno and the Paycock (Irish Repertory Theatre). She has appeared with most of the leading Irish repertory companies where productions included: Summer, The Plough and the Stars, The Shadow of a Gunman.
Television includes: Spencer for Hire, Rage of Angels, Juno and the Paycock.

Bronagh Gallagher
Theatre includes: A Crucial Week in the Life of a Grocer's Assistant, The Iceman Cometh, The Patriot Game (Abbey Theatre, Dublin); The Rocky Horror Show (SFX); Peer Gynt (world tour).
Television includes: Ruffian, You Me and Marley, The Bill, Flash McVeigh, The Shadow of a Gunman.
Film includes: Mary Reilly, The Commitments, Island of Strangers, Over the Rainbow, Pulp Fiction.

Tom Hickey
Theatre includes: Miss Julie, Antigone, Uncle Vanya, The Night of the Iguana (Dublin Focus); The Goodbye Machine (Project Art Gallery); Of Mice and Men, The Silver Dollar Boys, I Do Not Like Thee Doctor Fell, Observe the Sons of Ulster Marching Towards the Somme, Misogynist, The Great Hunger, The Gigli Concert; The Bearded Lady, Rise up Lovely Sweeney, Dance For Your Daddy, Snow White

(Abbey Theatre, Dublin); Heartbreak House, Waiting For Godot, Aristocrats, Three Sisters, The Double Dealer, A Midsummer Night's Dream, London Assurance, She Stoops to Conquer, Dorian Gray, Great Expectations (Gate, Dublin); The Kiss, The Gay Detective (Projects Art Centre); Juno and the Paycock, Three Sisters (RNT); Desire under the Elms (Greenwich).
Television includes: The Riordans, Roses from Dublin, The Year of the Child, One of Ourselves, Valentine Falls, Unnatural Pursuits, Against All Odds, Shannongate, Seachange.
Film includes: Flight of the Doves, Cal, To the Western World, Desecration, Gothic, High Spirits, My Left Foot, Nuns on the Run, Big Swinger, Fools of Fortune, The Miracle, Raining Stones, Circle of Friends.

Garry Hynes (director)
Garry Hynes founded Druid Theatre Company with Mick Lally and Marie Mullen in 1975, and was Artistic Director of the company from 1975-1990. She was Artistic Director of the Abbey Theatre, Dublin 1991-1994.
For the Royal Court: The Beauty Queen of Leenane (co produced with Druid).
Theatre includes: The Playboy of the Western World, Bailegangaire, Conversations on a Homecoming, Wood of the Whispering, Tis Pity She's A Whore, Poor Beast in the Rain (Druid); A Whistle in the Dark, King of the Castle, The Plough and the Stars, The Power of

Darkness, Famine (Abbey, Dublin); The Man of Mode, Song of the Nightingale (RSC); The Colleen Bawn (Royal Exchange Manchester). Garry was appointed Consultant Artistic Director to Druid in October 1994. She has recently been appointed an Assoicate Director at the Royal Court.

Des Keogh
Recent theatre includes, in the USA: The Best of Friends, The Gravity of Honey, Someone Who'll Watch Over Me, Forty-Four Sycamore, Dancing at Lughnasa.
In Ireland: The Plough and the Stars, Canaries, The Stanley Parkers , The Hostage.
Television includes: A variety of shows in Ireland and the UK, One-man shows in Ireland, the UK, Canada, the USA, the West Indies and Australia.
Film includes: Ulysses, Ryan's Daughter, Philadelphia Here I Come!. Solo performances at National Concert Hall, Dublin, Radio City Music Hall and Carnegie Hall, New York.
Radio includes Music for Middle Brows, RTE since 1968.

Marion O'Dwyer
Theatre includes: The Only True History of Lizzie Finn, Wonderful Tennessee (Abbey Theatre, Dublin and Plymouth Theatre); Dancing at Lughnasa (Abbey and Gaiety Theatres, Dublin, Sydney Opera); Moving, The Silver Tassie, You Can't Take It With You (Abbey Theatre,

Dublin); Pride and Prejudice, The Threepenny Opera, Our Country's Good, An Ideal Husband, Twelfth Night, Fathers and Sons (Gate Theatre, Dublin); Poor Beast in the Rain, Lovers' Meeting, The Donohue Sisters (Druid); Juno and the Paycock (Gaiety Theatre and Chicago).
Television and film includes: Finbar's Class, The Governor, The Life of Reilly, Secret of Ireland's Eye.
Radio: Marion was a member of the RTE Players for four years.

Stella McCusker
For the Royal Court: Pygmies in the Ruins
Other theatre includes: She Stoops to Conquer, The Playboy of the Western World, A Streetcar Named Desire, The Glass Menagerie (Lyric, Belfast); Brighton Beach Memoirs, The Year of the Hiker (Gaiety); The House of Bernarda Alba, Juno and the Paycock (Gate, Dublin and Broadway); At the Black Pig's Dyke (Druid), performed at the Edinburgh Festival, Toronto Festival Canada and Tricycle Theatre, Kilburn); Philadelphia, Here I Come!, The Mai (Abbey Theatre, Dublin and National tour); Donny Boy, The Beggar's Opera (Royal Exchange, Manchester); Ibsen's Ghosts (National Theatre, Oslo); Medea (Wyndhams).
Television includes: Aunt Suzanne, Naming the Names, Foreign Bodies, So You Think You've Got Troubles, You, Me and

Marley, Lovejoy, Act of Betrayal, Troubles, Errors and Omissions, Dear Sarah (winner of Jacobs Award). Film includes: The Playboys, Snakes and Ladders, Into the Sea, Mia Forever.

Jim Simmons
(lighting designer)
For the Royal Court: Uganda, Some Voices, Land of the Living. Other lighting designs include: The Winter's Tale, Anna Christie, All My Sons, The Snow Queen, Measure for Measure, Waiting for Godot, The Glass Menagerie, Sex Please We're Italian, All My Days, In the Midnight Hour (Young Vic); The Last Yankee (Young Vic & Duke of York's); Poppy, A, Love on the Plastic, Volpone, Spend Spend Spend, Dracula, Macbeth, Every Black Day, El Sid (Half Moon); Twelfth Night, Volpone (Birmingham Rep); World Storytime (Stratford East); Thatcher's Women (Tricycle); Blood Brothers (Liverpool, Tel Aviv, Lyric Shaftesbury Avenue); Sweeney Todd (Liverpool Playhouse, Watford, Half Moon); Having a Ball (Comedy); The Little Sister (Plymouth); Germinal, Pinocchio Boys (Paines Plough); Pericles, The Two Gentlemen of Verona, The Merry Wives of Windsor, As You Like It (RSC); Macbeth, Oliver, Sweeney Todd (Varmlands Opera Company, Sweden); Deborah's Daughter (Library Theatre, Manchester); Brecht in Hollywood (Moving Theatre); Song of an

Honourary Soulman (Smilin' Mongoose Theatre Co); Pinchi Kobi and the Seven Duppies (The Posse); The Sleeping Garden (Major Road). He has also worked in Holland, Belgium, Sweden, Norway, Israel and Germany and has designed over 30 shows for both Everyman & Playhouse Theatres in Liverpool.

Sean Rocks
For the Royal Court: Frank Pig Says Hello. Other theatre includes: The Silver Tassie (Abbey Theatre, Dublin); The Cuchulainn Cycle, Dierdre, Shadowy Waters, The Adventures of Shay Mouse (Peacock Theatre, Dublin); A Midsummer Night's Dream (Gate Theatre, Dublin); The Blue Macushla (Druid) The Cure at Troy (Field Day, Irish tour and the Tricycle Theatre, London); As You Like It, King Lear, The Merchant of Venice (Second Age); The Borstal Boy (Gaiety Theatre); Snow White (Olympia); Pentecost (Rough Magic Theatre Co.)
Television includes: Glenroe, Fair City, Dear Sarah, Go Now.

Don Wycherley·
Theatre includes: The Last Apache Reunion, The Honey Spike (The Abbey, Dublin); The Winter Thief (Peacock Theatre, Dublin); He made his debut at the Peacock in Away Alone. He has worked with Garry Hynes on two previous occasions - Famine, and The Crucial Week in the Life of a Grocer's Assistant (Abbey Theatre, Dublin).

Other appearances at the Abbey include The Comedy of Errors and Silverlands. He was in the most recent revival of Borstal Boy (Gaiety), and Bouncers (Tivoli).
Film and television includes: Widow's Peak, Kidnapped,Michael Collins (soon to be released), Last of the High Kings, Father Ted.

The Royal Court and the Abbey Theatres would like to thank the following for their help with this production: Ray McBride; Richmond Marketing; Aqua Libra; Benson and Hedges; Finches;Coca-Cola; Greengage Marketing Department; M.O'Brien (Hire and Catering Ltd.); Weirs Jewellers; Irish Wheelchair Association; Cantrell & Cochrane Ltd.; Stage Services North; Mr. Paul Wiseman; Joan Quinlivan; Debbie Vard; NEC; Tom Ryan; Rathbourne Candles; Justin Knee Shae; The Plough bar; Tipperary Water; McCabes Wine Merchants; Wardrobe care by Persil and Comfort courtesy of Lever Brothers Ltd, watches by The Timex Corporation, refrigerators by Electrolux and Philips Major Appliances Ltd.; kettles for rehearsals by Morphy Richards; video for casting purposes by Hitachi; backstage coffee machine by West 9; furniture by Knoll International; freezer for backstage use supplied by Zanussi Ltd 'Now that's a good idea.' Hair styling by Carole at Moreno, 2 Holbein Place, Sloane Square 0171 730 0211; Closed circuit TV cameras and monitors by Mitsubishi UK Ltd. Natural spring water from Wye Spring Water, 149 Sloane Street, London SW1, tel. 0171-730 6977. Overhead projector from W.H. Smith; Sanyo U.K for the backstage microwave.

The Opportunity of a Lifetime

On September 22, 1995 the Arts Council of England announced that the Royal Court Theatre was to be the recipient of a £16 million Lottery Fund Award. This award has provided the Court with a **once-in-a-lifetime** opportunity to bring this beautiful and important theatre up to date.

The refurbishment will touch all parts of the building, improving facilities for audiences and performers alike. The architects have prepared plans which retain the charm of the historic interior and facade of the Theatre, and the final result is a scheme which will *drastically improve* one of Britain's foremost producing theatres.

However the rules are clear; the Lottery Fund will pay up to three quarters of the costs of our £21 million capital project but the Royal Court must find the remainder itself as Partnership Funding.

This is a challenge we have readily accepted and we are talking with businesses, trust funds and private individuals throughout the country and internationally. Most recently the **New Yorker Magazine** and the **Conde Nast Foundation (USA)** have expressed a commitment to our fund-raising appeal.

In addition, David Suchet has spearheaded a drive which has raised substantial funds from our Friends and audience members. A **tremendous thank-you** to everyone who has generously supported this appeal through single gifts, gift aid and covenanted donations.

> *The name of the Royal Court Theatre is synonymous with freshness, dynamism and vibrancy and its world-wide reputation, for identifying and nurturing talent, is uncontested. As the millennium approaches and our visions of the future take shape, the Theatre is confident that its challenge to raise £5 million towards refurbishing its 100-year old home will be met by vigour, inspiration and conviction.*

For information on how you can play a part in securing our future please call **Jacqueline Simons**, Development Manager, on 0171-823-4132, while for a tour of the theatre before the redevelopment call **Josephine Campbell** on 0171-730-5174.

PORTIA COUGHLAN

for Dermot

First published in 1996
by Faber and Faber Limited
3 Queen Square London WC1N 3AU

Photoset by Parker Typesetting Service, Leicester
Printed in England by Clays Ltd, St Ives plc

Marina Carr is hereby identified as author of this work in accordance with
Section 77 of the Copyright, Designs and Patents Act 1988

All professional and amateur rights in this play are strictly reserved and
applications for permission to perform them must be made in advance,
before rehearsals begin to The Agency (London), Limited, 24 Pottery Lane,
Holland Park, London W11 4LZ. No performance may be given without
first obtaining permission.

A CIP record for this book
is available from the British Library
ISBN 0-571-19023-5

2 4 6 8 10 9 7 5 3 1

Characters

Portia Coughlan, thirty
Gabriel Scully, fifteen, Portia's twin, a ghost
Raphael Coughlan, thirty-five, Portia's husband, has a limp
Marianne Scully, fiftyish, Portia's mother
Sly Scully, fiftyish, Portia's father
Maggie May Doorley, fiftyish, Portia's aunt, Marianne's sister
Senchil Doorley, fiftyish, Maggie May's husband
Blaize Scully, eighty, Portia's grandmother
Stacia Diyle (the Cyclops of Coolinarney), thirty, Portia's friend
Damus Halion, thirtyish, Portia's lover
Fintan Goolan, thirtyish, the barman of the High Chaperal

Setting
The play is set in the Belmont Valley in the Midlands. The stage must incorporate three spaces: the living room of Portia Coughlan's house, the bank of the Belmont River, the bar of the High Chaperal.

Time
The present.

Glossary

Lewin	= Popping out of
Naggin	= Dram or tot
Cines	= Coins
Talche	= Talk
Thinche	= Think
Yar	= Your
Wache	= Week
Lave	= Leave
Grake	= Greek
Bilt	= Belt

Act One

SCENE ONE

Two isolating lights up. One on Portia Coughlan in her living room. She wears a nightdress and a sweatshirt. Dishevelled and barefoot, she stands staring forward, a drink in her hand, curtains closed. The other light comes up simultaneously on Gabriel Scully, her dead twin. He stands at the bank of the Belmont River singing. (Music to be decided.) They mirror one another's posture and movements in an odd way, unconsciously. Portia stands there drinking, lost-looking, listening with a terrible longing to Gabriel's voice.

Enter Raphael Coughlan, Portia's husband. He has a limp. He stands there unnoticed by Portia, watching her, car keys dangling, portable phone. As soon as he speaks Gabriel's song stops and lights fade on him.

Raphael Ah for fuche's sache.

Portia turns to look at him, looks away, takes another drink.

Tin a'clache i'tha mornin' an' ya'are ah ud arready.

Portia Though' you war ah worche.

Raphael Ah war.

Portia Cem bache ta cheche an me.

Raphael Noh especialla. (*Holds up brandy bottle, examines level, looks at her.*) An there's dishes i'tha kitchen as hasn't seen a drop of waher this weeche nor more.

Portia So.

I

Raphael An' tha kids, ya didn drive thim ta school in thah geh up ah hope.

Portia (*lighting a cigarette*) Stacia brun' thim.

Raphael Did tha have their breakfas'?

Portia A cuurse tha did, what ya tache me for ah all.

Raphael Jus' axin' Portia.

Portia Well don't arrigh'! An' if yar thah worriet about thim why'd'n ya mine thim yarself!

Raphael An' you'll go ouh an earn tha mona?

Portia If ya never med another penny we'd still be rich . . . Tae?

Raphael Naw.

Portia Busy ah tha factoray?

Raphael Aye.

Portia Ud's me birtha taday.

Raphael Thah so?

Portia Thirty . . . half me life's over.

Raphael Me heart goes out ta ya.

Portia Have wan wud me . . . an me birtha. (*A drink.*)

Raphael Ah this hour, ya mus' be ouha yar mine.

Portia pours one for herself defiantly.

Portia Slainte.

Raphael takes package from his pocket, throws it to her.

Raphael This be why ah chem bache this mornin'. Happa birtha Portia.

Portia Though' ya forgoh.

Raphael Did ya now.

Portia opens package. A vulgar diamond bracelet: sort of dismayed at its flashiness, her taste is better.

Portia Diamonds.

Raphael Why noh.

Portia Thanks Raphael . . . ud's lovela. (*Stands there looking at it.*)

Raphael Portia?

Portia Whah.

Raphael Wha's wrong a' ya?

Portia Natin'.

Raphael Natin' . . . well ah'd behher geh bache. Puh thah someways safe, ater settin' me bache five gran'. (*Bracelet. And exit Raphael.*)

Sound of Gabriel's voice begins again, Portia listens a minute, puts on CD to drown out voice, turns it up, Gabriel's voice subsides. Exit Portia.

SCENE TWO

Enter Maggie May Doorley, an old prostitute, black mini skirt, black tights, white high heels, sexy blouse, loads of costume jewellery, fag in her mouth, she carries a large parcel. Followed by Senchil Doorley, her husband, half the size of her, skinny, fussy, lovely.

Senchil (*following her, half dance, half run*) Leh me carry thah peh.

3

Maggie M (*talking through the fag*) S'arrigh' peh, ah have ud, anaways didn' tha doctor say as ya've ta mine yar heart. (*Calls.*) Portia!

Senchil Ya sure now peh? (*parcel*)

Maggie M Am peh.

Senchil (*indicating parcel*) Here puh thah down peh.

Maggie M S'arrigh' peh, Portia!

Senchil Don' strain yar vice peh.

Maggie M Arrigh' peh. PORTIA! Tache tha cigareh ouha me mouh, stingin' tha sockets a' me eyes.

Senchil (*takes cigarette out of her mouth*) Ya want another puff afore ah puh ud ouh peh?

Maggie M Aye. (*Takes a puff.*) Ah wonder is ahe gone.

Senchil Her char's ouhside anaways, sih down peh, yar varicoses, ya shouldn' be wearin' thim high hales peh, don' know ha mana times ah toult ya thah.

Maggie M Portia!

Portia (*off*) Whah?

Senchil She's here peh.

Maggie M On'y yar aul aunt.

Portia Sihdown ah'll be ouh in a minuhe.

Maggie M Ligh' us a cigareh there Senchil.

Senchil (*lighting one fussily*) Yar smochin' too much Maggie May an' ya didn' get yar lungs checked ouh this five year.

Maggie M Ah will, ah will peh.

Senchil Whin?

Maggie M Soon, soon.

Senchil Ah'm tiret machin' appintmints for ya now, Maggie May.

Maggie M Ah know y'are peh, an' sure why wouldn' ya be.

Senchil Sa long as ya know ah'm noh ta be tachen avantage of Maggie May, now.

Maggie M (*not listening to him, smoking away*) Ah know peh.

Senchil An' yar no use ta me dead Maggie May an' thah's tha truh of ud now.

Maggie M Noh a sign a' me dyin' Senchil, noh a sign.

Enter Portia, dressed in skirt, sandals, jumper. The same outfit for Acts One and Three.

There y'are.

Portia (*kisses Maggie May*) How'ya Senchil?

Senchil Ah'm vera well thanche ya Portia an' yarself, beauhiful day, beauhiful, beauhiful, a day ta seh tha bull amon tha heifers, a day ta hop tha ram in an tha ewes.

Maggie M (*looking at him*) Aye if there war era bull or a ram around, Portia for yar birthday. (*Hands her parcel.*)

Portia Ah there war no nade Maggie May.

Maggie M A Godchile's a Godchile, thah righ' Senchil?

Senchil Is peh.

Portia Whah is ud?

Senchil Open an' see now for yarself.

Portia takes a three-foot white delft horse on its hind legs from wrapping.

Portia (*laughs*) God Ammighy, ah may jump up an him an' ride off an him wan a' these days.

Maggie M Sem as a though' meself whin ah seen him.

Senchil Goh him ah tha garden cintre.

Portia Ah love ud Maggie May, yar fierce good ta me. (*Kisses her.*)

Maggie M Oh Senchil puh in for ud too.

Senchil Will ah mache a chup a tae peh?

Maggie M Mache wan for yarself peh, ah'll have a branda if Portia offers me wan.

Portia A cuurse ya will.

Senchil (*takes a packet of digestives from his pocket, offers them around*) Y'all have wan Portia?

Portia Ah won't Senchil.

Maggie M No thanks peh.

Senchil Ya don' mine me brinin' me own biscuits do ya now Portia?

Maggie M An' why would she peh, sure don't Portia know yar heart be banjaxed.

Senchil Ya see, sem as ah war t'ahe a chocolah biscuih an' sem as tha crumb a' tha chocolah turnt inta a cloh an' sem as thah vera cloh wint up ta me heart. (*Pregnant pause.*) A goner.

Maggie M Stiche ta yar digestives Senchil, tha's all ah'll say an tha mahher.

Senchil Ah will peh, ah will. (*Exits.*)

Maggie M Fierce down in yarself Portia.

6

Portia (*drinking*) Am ah?

Maggie M For a birtha ghirl an' all.

Portia Ah.

Maggie M Raphael tratin' y'arrigh'?

Portia Aye.

Maggie M Glad ta hear ud, an' tha kids?

Portia Sure they're nearla min, Jason be twelve chome Dicimber, Peher tin an' Quintin's in school arreada . . . had thim too young Maggie May . . . marriet ah seventeen, Jay whah war ah ah?

Maggie M Ah know peh.

Portia An' ah mimber ya tellin' me an' all.

Maggie M Nowan ever tachen my advice yeh, barrin Senchil, an' looche ah tha stahe a' him . . . mebbe ya war behher off, married ta wan a' tha richest min in tha counta, beauhiful house, beauhiful clothes, beauhiful everthin'.

Portia An ah was goin' ta college, had me place an' all, buh Daddy says naw, marry Raphael.

Maggie M Aul' Sly Scully, never liked him, God forgimme talchin' abouh yar father liche thah.

Portia Don't chare for him naither.

Maggie M Turnt yar mother agin me this years now.

Portia Mother . . . she war allas fierce wache.

Maggie M She warn't allas Portia, me an' her had greah times tagether, we'd paint tha town regular. Atwane yar father an' his aul' mother tha beah everthin' worth batin' ouh of her. Thah an' losin' her son.

Portia Yeah.

Enter Senchil, sound of Gabriel's voice comes over.

Maggie M Ya med yar tae peh.

Senchil Ah did peh, ya want me ta do tha washin' up Portia.

Portia Whah? (*Gabriel's song has taken her away.*)

Senchil Tha washin' up.

Portia Jay no Senchil, ud's gran', lave ud.

Maggie M Senchil's mighy ah tha washin' up.

Senchil Ah do love ud, loochin' ouh tha winda ah Maggie May's Arfrichan marigolds an' washin' tha ware, don'nen ah peh?

Maggie M Ya do.

Portia This lamb of a day an' me stuche here for all eterniha. Ah have ta geh ouh Maggie May.

Maggie M Chome inta town wud us.

Senchil Aye do.

Portia Ah thinche ah'll go walchin', pull tha duur ater ye. (*Exit Portia.*)

Senchil Bye peh.

Maggie M Quare mood.

Senchil Lonela in herself isn' she now Maggie May peh?

Maggie M She is.

Senchil Ah hope now if you was ever ta geh lonela an' fierce basement down in yarself, ah hope ya'd have tha dacenca ta tell me.

8

Maggie M Cuurse ah would peh.

Senchil An' ah'd have ya righ' as rain ere long.

Maggie M Ya would peh. Will we go or will ah have another wan? (*Drink.*)

Senchil Too erla peh.

Maggie M Don' start wan a yar lectures an drinchin' peh, chan't abide thim.

Senchil Ah won't peh, ah won't ona ud's no good for ya, branda for breakfas' an' me ater choochin' tha full fri for ya. D'ya thinche would y'ahe ud, noh a bih a' ya, had ta peg ud ta tha chah.

Maggie M Peh! Peh! Shu'p! Shu'p!

Senchil (*following her*) Manners Maggie May! Manners!

SCENE THREE

Enter Damus Halion, swarthy, handsome. By the bank of the Belmont River, he picks a clump of violets, arranges them into a bunch.
   Enter Portia.

Damus (*kisses her, puts a violet in her hair*) For tha birtha ghirl. (*Flowers. Stands back, admires her.*) Ya'll soon be an aul hag Portia Coughlan.

Portia Don't seem ta deter you none anaways.

Damus Whah tooche ya sa long?

Portia (*sitting on bank*) Visitors.

Damus Ah says ta meself aither she's gone offa me agin or aul Hop-along's finalla found ouh.

9

Portia Ah toult ya noh ta call him Hop-along! Chan't abide ud! S'noh hes fault half hes fooh was cuh off.

Damus Well there's mana as says he done ud be purpose for tha chompensation.

Portia All lies an' ya know ud, who in their righ' mine'd cuh off their fooh for a few quid?

Damus Ah know plinty as may for half a million, buh ah find yar difince a' yar husband touchin' an' a wee bit sintimintal. Coughlan if ya war mine an' ya talkt abouh me tha way ya talche abouh thah excuse of a man a' yourn ah'd chop yar head off an' ahe ud for me tae.

Portia Well ah'm noh yours nor anawan ilses Damus Halion.

Damus A'ya noh now.

Portia Gis a cigareh. (*He lights one for her, she lies back and smokes.*) Lovela here.

Damus (*kisses her, a long lusty kiss*) C'man up ta tha boah house.

Portia In a minuh.

Damus Ah've ta be bache in an hour.

Portia Then go if yar worried.

Damus Wan a yar bitchy moods agin.

Portia Ah mane, for Jaysus sache Damus, chan't we jus' sih an' talche or d'ya noh wanta talche ta me. Why does ud allas have ta be thrashin' an' sweatin' i'tha boah house?

Damus Missus, ud was you gev me tha chome an an' now ya wanta talche.

Portia Ta my reckonin', bin a long time since ah gev you anathin' approachin' a chome an.

Damus Thah a fac' . . . (*Lies back, sucking grass.*) Whah kapes ya chomin' here so?

Portia Ah chome here because ah've allas chome here an' ah reckon ah'll be chomin' here long ater ah'm gone. Ah'll lie here whin ah'm a ghos' an' smoche ghos' cigarettes an' watch ye earthlin's goin' abouh yeer pintless days.

Damus Yar cracked as yar twin.

Portia An you're as thiche as tha rest a' thim. Though' ah'd tache ya ouha tha slime buh ud's still drippin' offa ya.

Damus Wasn' far from slime ya was reared yarself Portia Coughlan. Yar aunt tha village bike! Yar father gettin' aul Tim Lahane drunche an' stalin' hees land offa him.

Portia Me father bought thah land fair an' square.

Damus Aye an' Tim Lahane scuttered under tha table an' he signin' ud over, never a soult ud an' him sober.

Portia Ya don' know whah yar talchin' anouh so kape yar big thiche mouh shuh 'till ya do.

Damus Yar more trouble nor anathin' else Portia Coughlan, allas war, led me a dance this years. Wance ud was me ya war goin' ta marry buh ah warn't good enough war ah, wance ya clapt yar greeda eyes an Raphael Coughlan wud hees big char an hees big factora an' pound signs lewin' in hees eyes.

Portia Tha's righ', geh ud offa yar chest, ya'll fale behher. Jaysus yar so fuchin' bihher!

Damus Noh exactla a picture a bliss yarself, looche ah ya.

Portia Yar righ' ah'm noh continted an' have'n bin this long while gone.

Damus C'man tha boah house, there's still time.

Portia Ah have ta go.

Damus Tomorra.

Portia If ah fale liche ud. (*Throws flowers into river, and exiting.*)

Damus Ah don' know whah ud is ya want from me.

Portia Ah don' know aither.

Damus Fuche ya! (*Exits.*)

SCENE FOUR

Enter Portia and the cyclops, Stacia. They sit at the bar of the High Chaperal.

Stacia An' Quintin was ballin' hees eyes ouh, had ta drag him from tha char inta tha classroom.

Portia (*barely listening*) Fierce difficult, Quintin.

Stacia He's on'y a childt Portia, ya may go softer an him.

Enter **Fintan,** *the barman of the High Chaperal, cowboy ankle boots, jeans.*

Fintan Ladies yees are lookin' extremla beauhiful this sultra summer's day.

Stacia Ud's Portia's birtha.

Portia Now's yar excuse ta gimme a khiss. (*Proffers cheek.*)

Fintan G'way ouha thah wud yar cheeche. Cheeche's is for grannys an' aul' spinster aunts. Ah ona ever khisses women an tha lips nor tha legs.

Stacia D'ya hare him, tha cheeche a'ya!

Portia (*offers leg*) Be tha leg so, me lips is Raphael's, God help him.

The leg is kissed.

G'way now an' lave me leg alone afore ya swally ud.

Fintan Ah've swallyed worser.

Stacia A bottle a cider Fintan, an' Portia whah're ya havin'?

Portia Sem as ever.

Fintan Branda an' ginger chomin up.

Stacia Fierce forrard isn' he now? Whah d'ya thinche a' me new eye-patch Portia?

Portia Suits ya.

Stacia Pigskin. Goh four a thim, wan's blue, wan's grane, wan's yella an' wan's blache for mass an' funerals. Sint away t'Englan' for thim.

Portia Ah don' know Stacia, sometimes ah thinche if ah had me eye gouged ouh ah'd wear nera patch ah all.

Stacia Ah no Portia, ud'd frighten tha children, as ud is they're a bih ashamed a' me.

Portia Pihy abouh thim.

Enter Fintan with drinks.

Fintan An tha house ladies, a sourta birtha present, whah age a'ya anaways?

Stacia Ya know well whah age she is, ya'd know less an' you a class ahind her in Miss Sullivan's school. Yar ona machin' small talche so as ya chan ogle her over.

Fintan D'ya know whah ud is Stacia Diyle, you're gettin' more observant since ya lost th'eye.

Stacia All tha behher ta see through you wud Fintan Goolan. Have ya no worche ta be doin' instead a sniffin' 'roun' tha skirts a' two marriet women.

Fintan Don't overestimate yarself Stacia Diyle whin ud chomes ta my attentions an' for yar information, ah never sniffs where there an't a scent. (*Looks at Portia and exits.*)

Stacia Kape away from him Portia, bad news, bad news.

Portia Ah he's on'y jossin' us, yar too serious Stacia.

Stacia Ah'm tellin' ya now Portia, thah fella'd have ya pillowed an' then broadchast ud an tha mornin' news, goh a cousin a' mine up tha pole las' year, denied ud ta tha hilt. Ah don' liche him wan bih.

Portia Cheers anaway. (*Drinks and smokes.*)

Stacia Raphael tachin' y'ouh ta celebrahe tanigh'?

Portia Celebrahe . . . Me an' Raphael . . . (*Laughs.*) Chan't imagine ud.

Stacia He noh tachin' y'ouh for dinner or somethin'?

Portia Nah, we're pas' thah kinda larche, lasteways ah am.

Stacia God, Justin an' me goes ouh regular, ya nade time be yeerselves Portia.

Portia An' whah d'yees talche abouh, yarself an' Justin, whin ye'er be yeerselves.

Stacia Whah d'ya mane, whah do we talche abouh?

Portia Ah mane, be there ana differ sittin' opposite him wud a chandle stuche atwane yees than there would be if yees war ah home facin' wan another in armchairs.

Stacia A cuurse there be.

Portia Asplaine ud ta me thin, whah tha differ be.

Stacia Well jay, dunno if ah chould righly say whah ud is.

Portia These days ah looches ah Raphael sittin' opposite me i'tha armchair. He's allas tired, hees bad leg up an a stool, addin' up tha booches from tha factora, lost in heeself, an' ah thinches tha pair of us migh' as well be dead for all tha jiy we knoche ouha wan another. Tha kids is aslape, tha house creachin' liche a choffin, all thim wooden duurs an' fluurs, sometimes ah chan't brathe anamore.

Stacia Ya nade ta do more things Portia, geh ouha tha house, geh away from thah river, why'd'n ya geh him ta tache ya an a holida. Whin's tha las' time ya had a holida?

Portia An't never bin an wan Stacia.

Stacia Jay tha's righ, y'ant never had a holida. Tha's shochin' Portia! Shochin'!

Portia Don' want wan, don' thinche ah'd survive a nigh' away from tha Belmont valla.

Stacia Don' be daft, a cuurse ya would, migh' aven enjiy ud.

Portia Oh ah'm sure ah'd live through whah other folks calls holida's buh me mind'd be turnin' an tha Belmont River. Be wonderin' war ud flowin' rough or smooth, was tha banche mucky nor dry, was tha salmon beginnin' their rowin' for tha sae, was tha frogs spawnin' tha waher lilies, had tha heron returned, be wonderin' all a these an' a thousan' other wonderin's thah river washes over me.

Stacia Ah know Portia, ah know.

Portia (*empties her glass*) Another?

Stacia (*checks her watch*) School's neara over, kids'll be waitin', jus' go ta tha loo.

Exit Stacia. Sound of Gabriel, faint. Enter Fintan.

Fintan Ya chould kape behher compana nor tha cyclops a Coolinarney.

Portia Don' chall her thah i'front a' me an' if ya want ta screw me Fintan Goolan, have tha dacenca t'ax me liche a man 'stead a' fussin' 'roun' me liche an auld cluchin' hin!

Fintan Fierce sure a' yarself, an't ya.

Portia Ah seen ya loochin', nigh an ever' time ah chome in here.

Fintan Have ya now?

Portia An' ya know ud, wide boy.

Fintan Well ah'm free this evenin'.

Portia Ah bet y'are . . . Seven . . . tha Belmont River.

Fintan Ah'll tache ya for dinner.

Portia Chan have dinner ah home, on'a want ta fuche ya, fine ouh if yar ana good whahever thah manes, see if there's anathin' ahind a' thah cowbiy swagger an' too-honeyed tongue.

Exit Portia. Stacia returns, goes up to Fintan.

Stacia Loochin for somewhere ta puh ud Goolan? (*flips up eye-patch*) G'wan ah dare ya, ah fuchen dare ya. (*Exit Stacia.*)

Fintan (*looking after her*) Jaysus H! (*Exits.*)

SCENE FIVE

Enter Gabriel Scully, he wanders by the Belmont River, singing. Effect must be ghostly.

16

Portia is in her living room, eyes closed. Leaning against the door, listening. Hold a while. Doorbell rings. No move from Portia. Again. Still no move. And yet again, impatiently, aggressively, still no move.

Marianne Scully, Portia's mother, appears, watches Portia leaning against other door. Eyes closed.

Marianne So ya don' aven bother answerin' tha duur anamore.

Portia (*eyes closed still as song gets fainter and Gabriel drifts off*) Knew be tha witchy ring ud be yarself an' ya'd be bargin' in afore long acause ya never learnt, Mother, t'allow a person space an' quieh.

Marianne Wan a yar bad timpered moods agin. (*Begins tidying up.*) Tha stahe a' tha place, looche ah ud.

Portia Lave ud.

Marianne (*ignoring her, continuing tidying*) Ya'd sweer ya war never taugh' how ta hoover a room or dust a mantel. Bledy disgrace, tha's whah y'are. (*Shouts off.*) Sly chome an in she's here.

Tidying with impotent rage, Portia undoes what she does.

Marianne Will ya stop ud! An' wheer's yar children? Playin' 'roun' tha Belmont River ah suppose. You be luchy tha don' fall in an drown thimsilves wan a these days.

Portia Ya'd liche thah wouldn' ya, wapin' ah tha grave a' wan a' yar darlin' gran'sons. Be histora rapatin' udself, wouldn't ud now, be liche buryin' Gabriel all over agin. Ah knows how your bihher mine works, ya thinche thah if wan a' my sons was drownt thah mebbe ya could asplaine away how me twin was lost. Well mother, natin'll ever asplaine thah, natin'.

Marianne Ah would ya stop such nonsinse, don' know whah yar talchin' abouh, yar so darche Portia, allas war.

Portia Ah rade subtext mother, words dropt be accident, phrases covered over, sintinces unfinished, an' ah know tha topography a' your mine as well as ah know ever' inch an' ditch an' drain a' Belmont Farm. So don't you bluster in here an' puh a death wish an my sons jus' acause ya couldn' save yar own. My sons'll be fine for if ah does natin' else ah lave thim alone an' no marche be behher than a blache wan.

Marianne Y'ave nera righ' remindin' me a' Gabriel in such a bleache an' blameful way.

Portia He woulda bin thirty taday as well . . . sometimes ah thinche on'y half a' me is left, tha worst half . . . D'ya know thon'y rason ah married Raphael? Noh acause you an' Daddy says ah should, noh acause he war rich, ah chare natin' for money, naw, thon'y rason I married Raphael was acause of hees name, a angel's name sem as Gabriel's, an' ah though' be osmosis or jus' pure wishin' thah wan'd tache an' tha qualihies a th'other. Buh Raphael is noh Gabriel an' never will be . . . An' ah dreamt abouh him agin las' nigh'. Was wan a' thim drames as is so rale ya thinche ud's actualla happenin'. Gabriel had chome ta dinner here an' ater he goh up ta lave an' ah says, 'Gabriel stay for tha weechind', an' Gabriel demurs ouha poliheness ta me an' Raphael. An' ah says, 'Gabriel, ud's me Portia, yar twin, don' be polihe, there's no nade wud me' . . . an' thin he turns an' smiles an' ah know he's gointa stay an' me heart blows open an' stars falls ouha me chest as happens in drames . . . we war so aliche, warn't we mother?

Marianne Tha spih, couldn't tell yees apart i'tha cradle.

Portia Chem ouha tha womb howldin' hands . . . whin

God war handin' ouh souls, he musta goh mine an'
Gabriel's mixed up, aither thah or he gev us jus' tha wan
atwane us an' ud wint inta tha Belmont River wud him
. . . Oh Gabriel ya had no righ' ta discard me so, ta floah
me an tha world as if ah war a ball a' flotsam, ya had no
righ' . . . (*Begins to weep uncontrollably.*)

Marianne Stop ud! Stop ud! Stop ud righ' now! (*Shakes
her.*) Thah's enough a' thah! If yar father hares ya! Control
yarself! If ya passed yar day liche any normal woman
there'd be none a' this! Stop ud! Stop ud! Ah'm warnin' ya
now!

    Enter Sly and Blaize.

Blaize Would ya lave me chair alone! Ya'll destriy me
braches.

Sly Marianne do somethin' wud thah wan, she have me
diminted.

Marianne Why'd'n ya lave her in tha char.

Sly Don'nen you start, Jaysus.

Marianne Y'arrigh' there Mrs Scully?

Blaize Am, Mrs Scully.

Sly Happa birtha Portia.

Blaize Birtha's . . . load a bollix!

Sly Toult ya Mammy, noh ta be cursin', chan'abide ud in
a woman.

Blaize An' ah toult you ah spint tha first eigh'y year a' me
life howldin' me tongue, fuchin' an' blindin' inta tha pilla,
an' if God sees fih ta gimme another eigh'y, tha'll be spint
spachin' me mine foul nor fair.

Sly Yar mother an' me Portia, seh a thinchin' whah'd

Portia liche for her birtha an' we rached out brains, didn' we Marianne?

Marianne We did.

Sly There be natin' tha ghirl nades nor wants was th'ony conclusion we could chome ta.

Blaize Sly havin' trouble partin' wud mona agin.

Marianne Wasn' from tha wind he learnt ud.

Blaize Swear ta Jaysus if hell war free ya'd go there, sooner nor pay a small intry free to heaven.

Sly Is there anathin' ya want Portia?

Portia Naw.

Sly See, toult ya, natin' tha ghirl nades nor wants Marianne.

Portia So yees jus' brun' yeeselves.

Marianne Seen a dress in tha boutiche yesterda, purple wud fleches a gold, toult ya we shoulda goh ud for her Sly.

Sly Then we'll geh ud for tha ghirl, Marianne, okhay, we'll geh ud.

Blaize C'man! Home!

Sly No yeh Mother.

Blaize If ah'd the power a me legs agin! Why won'nen yees lave me be me own anamore! Afeard ah'll fall inta tha fire, jus' wanted ta lie up agin tha range listenin' ta the Count John McCormacche, d'ya thinche would yees leh me! Fuche yees!

Portia pours a drink for herself.

Marianne Ah this hour! Sly!

Portia Yees know where tha duur is if'n yees chan stan' tha sigh' a' me . . . anawan chare ta jine me?

Sly Tae.

Portia Mache yarself ah home Daddy.

Marianne Ah'll mache ud seein as yar daughter haven tha manners ta.

And exit Marianne.

Sly Seen ya talchin' ta young Halion agin taday down be tha Belmont River.

Portia Spyin' an me agin.

Sly Goin' abouh me business mendin finces an tha shalla side. Portia whah're y'up ta wud him? He's no good thah fella, nor any he chem from.

Blaize Tha chount, p'an tha chount.

Sly Ah'm talchin' ta ya ghirl.

Portia He knew Gabriel.

Sly Gabriel, forgeh Gabriel, thah unnatural child thah shamed me an' yar mother so.

Portia Forgeh Gabriel . . . he's everwhere Daddy, everwhere. There's noh a corner a ana a' your forty fields thah don remine me a Gabriel. Hees name is in tha mouths a' tha starlin's thah swoops over Belmont Hill, tha cows bellow for him from tha barn an frosty winter nights. Tha very river tells me thah wance he was here an' now he's gone. An' you ax me ta forgeh him. Whin ah lie down ah th'en of another impossible day, ah pray for tha time . . . Daddy ya don' understan' natin'.

Sly Don' talche down ta me you. Ah've worked long an hard for you ta be where y'are taday, built Belmont Farm

21

up from twinty achre a' bog an' scrub ta wan a' tha fines' farms in tha county, wud thim there hands. Thah don' happen jus' liche thah! An d'ya thinche Raphael Coughlan'd've looched ah you twice if there warn't land an money goin' wud ya. An' for you ta be hangin' 'roun' tha liches a Damus Halion. Sur' thim Halions wouldn' geh ouha bed in tha mornin' ta milche tha cows. Scrubbers! Thah's all th'are, wouldn' know a heifer from a jachass.

Portia Daddy ah war on'y talchin' to him.

Sly More nor talchin' I seen. Ah'm tellin' ya now, puh a halter on thah wayward arse a yours.

Portia Ah'm siche a you gawkin' ah me from ahind hedges an ditches an sconces. Ah'm a grown woman an' whah ah do is none a' your concirn. (*Begins walking off, going to exit.*)

Sly Don'en you walche away whin ah'm talchin' ta ya! An ud's ever bih a my concirn whin ud chomes ta tha Scully name. Don'en ya know everwans watchin', bin watchin' us these years. Where's yar ehics ghirl, yar moralihy an yar ehics thah me an yar mother tried ta learn ya.

Blaize Tha chount John, where is he!

Enter Marianne with tea, as Portia goes to exit.

Marianne An' where a you off ta an' visihors in tha house.

Portia Visihors! Jaysus, permanent fixtures be more liche! (*And exit Portia.*)

Marianne Sometimes, Sly, ah do wonder be tha ghirl stable ah all?

Blaize Ah warnt ya an' ah toult ya Sly ta kape away from tha Jiyces a' Blacheion, tinkers tha loh a' thim.

Marianne We war never tinkers an' well you know ud.

Blaize Oh yes yees war! Cem inta this area three giniration ago wud natin' goin' for yees barrin' flamin' red hair an' fah arses. An' tha county council buildin' yees houses from our hard ernt monies. We don' know where ye chem from, tha histories a' yeer blood. Ah warnt ya Sly! D'ya thinche ya'd fuchin' listen! There's a divil in thah Jiyce blood, was in Gabriel, an' ud's in Portia too. God protec' us from thah blache-eyed gypsy tribe wud their blache blood an' their blache souls!

Marianne Ya goin' ta stan' there an' jus' leh her talche ta me liche thah!

Sly Ah now Marianne she don't mane ud.

Marianne She mane's ever bih of ud! An' whah war you afore ya war married? Wan a' tha ingrown inbred, scurvied McGoverns! Tha say yar father war yar brother!

Blaize Ya fuchin' tramp ya!

Sly Ah Jaysus women! Jaysus!

Blaize All a' tha McGoverns was bred fair an' square which be more nor ya chan say for tha Jiyces!

Sly Mother ah'm tellin' ya puh a fuchen lid an ud now!

Blaize Shu'p ta be fuched you!

Sly Arrigh' ah'm sayin' natin'! Khill wan another for all I cheer!

Blaize (*trying to get out of wheelchair*) You Missus!

Sly Thah's righ' Mother breache thah hip ah'm noh payin' for another wan!

Marianne She chome nare me an ah breache ud for her!

Blaize (*leaning forward in chair*) Ah know whah's atin'

23

you an' ah've watched ud ahe tha very heart ouha ya this fifteen year!

Marianne Ya know natin'!

Blaize Ya kilt yar son! Yar beauhiful son who had a vice liche . . .

Marianne Ah never led a finger an him an well you know ud! Jus tryin' t'upseh me ya vicious evil minded yoche ya!

Blaize Ah fingers! Who's talchin' abouh fingers! Whin tha whole worldt knows ya can kill a body jus' be loochin' ah thim if ya looche long enough an' ya looche wrong enough! Ah know yar darche aul fuchin' Jiyce strake an' whah ud does to a . . .

Sly Mother thah's enough! Warnin' ya now!

Marianne Ah don' want her nex' nor nae me agin. Ya may tind her from here an in. Ah'll sih in me bedroom if ah have ta, tha way she med me do whin first ah war a bride. Amimber thah y'aul witch, sindin' me up ta me room whin all tha worche was done, an Portia an' Gabriel wud me. Six a' clache an' summer evenin's, sint ta tha room, tha sun shinin' as if ud war midday, acause ya couldn' bear ta share yar kitchen wud a Jiyce. An' you leh her an' kep yar head down, doin' yar farm booches, dramin' a' achres, an' whah good are tha ta ya now, ya've nowan ta lave thim ta, an' tha twins an' me above i'tha room, too hot ta slape, wonderin' whah ud was we'd done ta be banished from our own kitchen. (*Goes to exit.*)

Sly Marianne.

Marianne Don't chall me in thah vice Sly, sickens me this long time gone. Tache yar mother home an' mine her, tha way ya shoulda minded me an yar children, for we nade yar harsh chare namore. (*Exits.*)

Sly Fuchen happy now a'ya! Why chan'nen ya lave tha waman alone!

Blaize Tache me home ta John McCormacche an' don' worra abouh thah wan, tough as an aul boot, she be in tha duurway, po-faced, falin' sorry for sheself afore dusk.

SCENE SIX

Enter Raphael Coughlan. Calls.

Raphael Portia. (*No answer.*)

> *He begins tidying up the place. Puts on some music. Sets the table for two, lights candles. Opens bottle of wine. Let this go on simultaneously with what's happening by the Belmont River.*
>   *Enter Portia by the river. Smokes. Throws leaves into river. Dusk. An owl hoots. She sits on her hunkers looking into the river. Enter Fintan. Stands there. Watches her a while.*

Fintan Yar two hours lahe.

Portia (*up from a dream*) Whah?

Fintan Chem ah seven liche ya says.

Portia Oh righ'.

Fintan Couldn' geh away, ah says ta meself. Luchy ah chem bache. (*Takes out a naggin of whiskey.*) Whiskey?

Portia Why noh.

Fintan (*pours whiskey into two plastic cups*) Cheers.

Portia Aye.

Fintan Fierce close ta home . . . don'nen yar father's land go by this place?

25

Portia Aye . . . an' sur ah live on'y up tha lane.

Fintan Ya liche flyin' i'tha face a' everwan, do ya.

Portia If'n ya want tha hones' ta Jaysus truh Fintan ah forgoh all abouh ya. Ah chem down here acause ah allas chome down here.

Fintan Forgoh all abouh me! Ya mache ud vera hard for a man Portia Coughlan.

Portia (*barely listening*) Do ah.

Fintan Aye, ya do.

Puts a hand on her arm, she looks at the hand, he removes the hand.

Fierce quieh here.

Portia Ya chan hear tha salmon goin' up river if ya listen well enough, strugglin' for tha Shannon, an' up inta tha mouh a' tha sae an' from there a slow cruise home ta tha spawnin' grounds a' th'Indian Ocean.

Fintan Thah a fac.

Portia Tha never med thah journey afore, jus' born knowin' tha rouhe tha'll travel.

Fintan (*not one bit interested*) Fascinatin', fascinatin'.

Portia Ever hare tell a' how tha Belmont River chem ta be callt tha Belmont River.

Fintan Heerd tell arrigh', Miss Sullivan used ta tell us in school. Fuchen hahed English an all thah aul poehic shihe she used drum inta us . . . wasn' ud abouh some aul River God be tha nem a Bel an a mad hoor of a witch as was doin all sorts a avil 'roun' here buh tha fuchen puh her in her place, by Jaysus tha did.

Portia She warnt a mad hoor of a witch! An she warnt

26

avil, jus different is all, could tell the future, and the paple 'roun' here impaled her on a stache an lef her ta die. An Bel heard her cries an cem down tha Belmont Valley an tachen her away from here an the river was born. An tha say Bel tachen more nor tha ghirl whin he swept through tha valley, ah don know enough abouh thah buh ah thinche tha do say righ' for this place mus surela be tha dongeon a tha fallen worldt.

Fintan Tha whah.

Portia Gabriel used hare tha ghirl whin tha river war low, said she sounded liche a aria from a chave.

Fintan Load a bollix if'n y'ax me, thim aul stories.

Portia Ah'm noh axin ya.

Fintan There's wan story as interests me Portia Coughlan, tha story a you wud yar knickers off, now thah's a story ah'd listen ta for a while.

Portia Ya fuchen turnip head ya! Jus geh offa me father's land Fintan Goolan acause yar a fuchen clodhopper jus liche yar paple afore ya an liche those ya'll spawn after ya in a wet ditch an a weh nigh in a drunken stupor!

Fintan Y'ave a lug an ya Portia Coughlan thah'd turn bache a funeral! An' y'ave a tongue an ya thah if I ownt ya ah'd moe tha big shoh, stuche up bejaysus ouha!

Portia Ah'm noh afraid a' you. Sa don waste yar time threatenin' me . . . thinche ah'll wade home be tha river . . . Nigh'.

And exit Portia.

Fintan Fuchen mickey dodger! (*And storms off.*)

*Focus back on Raphael finishing bottle of wine. Candles
have burnt down. He walks around impatiently. Portia
appears in doorway, barefoot, carries her sandals, stands
there.*

Raphael An' where war ya 'till this hour?

Portia (*looks at table*) Tha chandles an' tha wine. (*Leans
against doorway wearily.*)

Raphael Aye . . . chooked dinner for ya an' all, spiilt now.

Portia Dinner . . . Tccch. (*Sighs.*)

Raphael Nigh an midnigh' Portia.

Portia Is ud.

Raphael Bin home sense seven, kids atin' rubbich an'
watchin' videos, no homeworche done, no lunch no dinner
in thim. Where war ya?

Portia Ah Raphael, lame me alone.

Raphael Quintin cryin' hes eyes ouh all evenin' for ya.

Portia He'll grow ouha me ivintualla. (*Dries her legs with
a cushion.*)

Raphael Ah for Jaysus sache Portia he's on'y four!

Portia Ah knows whah age he is an' ah want as little as
possible ta do wud him arrigh'! (*Pours the end of the wine
for herself, sits and smokes.*)

Raphael Yar own sons.

Portia Ah never wanted sons nor daughers an' ah never
pertended otherwise ta ya, toult ya from tha start. Buh ya
though' ya chould woo me inta motherhood. Well ud
hasn't worched ouh has ud. Y'ave yar three sons now so

ya behher mine thim acause ah chan't love thim Raphael, ah'm jus' noh able.

Raphael Portia ah know thah taday of all days yar down an' ah know why. Now ah don' mache ouh t'unnerstan' tha breadth an' dipth a' you an' Gabriel. Ah have heerd thah tha bond atwane twins be ever strange an' inexplicable, buh surela now ud's time ta lave ud go an' try ta mache yar life athouh' him.

Portia (*erupting, like a madwoman*) Gabriel! Gabriel! Ha dare you mention hees name! Tha problem's noh Gabriel, ah'm over him this years! Tha problem's you! Ah fuchin' hate ya! Moochin' up ta me wud yar sliche theories an wha's wrong a' me! Ya haven't a fuchen' clue y'igorant aul' fuchen' cripple ya! A chan't bear tha sigh' a' ya hobblin' 'roun' me wud yar bad fooh an' yar custom med cowbiy boots!

Raphael Stop! Portia! Stop! Stop!

Portia An' whin you touch me at nigh', sometimes ah've jus' goh slape, often tha firs slape a' weeches an' ah'm slidin' inta a dramc thah'll tache me away from this livin' hell an' you touch me an' lurch me bache ta Belmont Valla, an' times yar lucky ah don' rip ya ta pieces or plunge a breadknife through yar lily heart!

Raphael (*going over to her*) Portia ya don' mane ana a' this, yar upseh, ya chan't mane whah ya bin sayin.

Portia (*shaking with rage*) Geh away from me! Ya thinche ah don't! Then hare this an' le's be free of all illusions for evermore. Ah despise you Raphael Coughlan, wud yar limp an' yar chape suits an' yar slow ways! A chompletla an uhherla despise you for whah y'are in yarself, buh more for who ya will never be! Now lame me alone! An ligh' namore chandles for me for fear ah blinds ya wud thim! (*Snuffs out candles violently.*)

Raphael Portia please, don' spache ta me liche this, please thinche whah yar sayin', this isn' you . . .

Portia Tha fool chomes bache for more! Well there's more! Y'axed me where ah war tanigh', well now ah'll tell ya. Ah was screwin' tha barman from tha High Chaperal! Gettin' angra now a'ya? Good, beginnin' ta hate me, behher still. Ah want none a' yar wahery love Raphael Coughlan an' while we're an tha subjec' he war useless, jus' as ah knew he would be, useless, as useless as you! G'wan cry away, breache yar heart Raphael Coughlan, ud'll hale, don't worra, ud'll hale, an' ah'll go guarantor for you thah wance ud's haled there'll be natin' under sun or moon thah'll ever lance ud's tough hide agin.

Lights down.

Act Two

By the Belmont River. Evening. A search light swoops
around the river. Raphael, Marianne, Sly, Stacia, Damus,
Fintan, Senchil and Maggie May. They stand in silence as
a pulley raises Portia Coughlan out of the river. She is
raised into the air and suspended there, dripping water,
moss, algae, frog spawn, water lilies, from the river.
Gabriel Scully stands aloof on the other bank, in profile,
singing.
   Ensemble choreography.
   All take a step back in unison as Portia is raised from
the river.
   All stop in unison when pulley reaches its height.
   All take another step back in unison.
   All look up at the dead Portia in unison.
   Portia sways there, pulley creaking, Gabriel singing,
water dripping.

Marianne Oh no.

Maggie M Swate sufferin' Jaysus.

Senchil Will somewan for Chrissache cover her.

Portia wears only a slip. No one moves, transfixed by
the elevated image of the dead Portia. Senchil takes off
his jacket, tries to cover her, she's too high, jacket falls,
suspends on her foot, hangs there.
   Hold a couple of beats. Then lower pulley. Raphael
moves forward to take her in his arms. Fintan moves to
help.

Raphael (*a measured growl*) Kape yar paws offa my wife.

Fintan moves back. Sly Scully takes rope off pulley.
Portia is now free of pulley and in Raphael's arms.

Marianne Ud's happent agin! (*Begins beating Sly on the chest. He stands there frozen, allowing her, not registering the blows.*) Ud's happent agin an' ya toult me ud would never!

Sly puts arms around Marianne, allows her to beat him.

Oh Maggie May, whah have she gone an' done.

Raphael (*whispering*) Portia! Portia.

Maggie M Ah don' know peh, ah don' know.

Raphael Ah suppose ah may tache her up ta tha house. (*Looks around hopelessly.*) Whah?

Sly Ah.

Raphael begins moving off with Portia, stumbles, all stumble in response, intake of breath from Raphael, answered by intake of breath from the others. They follow him off. Fintan and Damus left looking after them. Fintan offers cigarette to Damus, they light them, stand there smoking in silence holding the lighted end of their cigarettes in close to the palm.
After a while.

Damus Strange bird allas . . . Portia Coughlan.

Fintan Aye.

Damus Tha twin too.

Fintan Aye.

Damus Aye.

Fintan Gabriel.

Damus Tha's righ'.

Fintan On'y fifteen.

Damus Exac' sem spoh he war pulled from too.

Fintan Thah a fac'.

Damus Lookt liche a ghirl.

Fintan Sang liche wan too.

Damus Aye . . . wan thin' ah allas foun strange abouh thim Scully twins.

Fintan Whah was thah?

Damus . . . ya'd ax thim a question an' tha'd boh answer tha sem answer . . . ah tha sem time, esac' inflexion, esac' pause, esac' everthin'.

Fintan Forgotton thah.

Damus Ya'd put thim in different rooms, still tha sem answer.

Fintan Aye . . . mimber now.

Damus Mimber tha school tour.

Fintan Which wan?

Damus Tha wan ta Behhy's Town.

Fintan Naw.

Damus Portia an' Gabriel sah up i'tha front a' tha bus in red shorts an' whihe tay shirts.

Fintan Aye.

Damus Whisperin' ta wan another as was their wont. We goh ta Behhy's Town, still have tha phoha a' tha whole class, still chan't tell wan a' thim from th'other . . . anaways whim tha time chem ta geh bache an' tha bus, Portia an' Gabriel was missin'. Mad search wint an, nera

33

sign a' thim, tha coastghuards callt in, helacopters, lifeboats, tha worches. Tha pair a thim found five mile ouh ta sae in a row boah. Tha jus' goh in an' started rowin'. Poor aul' Miss Sullivan in an awful stahe. 'Whah war yees ah children, whah war yees ah, ah all?' 'We war jus' goin' away' says wan a' thim. 'Away! Away where i' tha name a' God' says Miss Sullivan. 'Anawhere' says th'other a thim, 'jus anawheres thah's noh here.'

Fintan Anawheres tha's noh here, Jaysus.

Damus Aye.

Fintan Sur aul' Hop-alon chould never manage her.

Damus Lucha ta geh her, though ah wouldn't chare for hees shoes now.

Fintan Whah'd she ever see in him?

Damus Chould a' had anawan, Portia Coughlan.

Fintan Ah . . . she chould.

Damus Anawan . . . anawan.

   Both exit.

SCENE TWO

Lights up on Blaize and Stacia manoeuvring Blaize's wheelchair into Portia's living room.

Stacia A'ya arrigh' now?

Blaize Am Mrs Diyle thanche ya.

Stacia Ah'll lave ya here so, an' geh th'aheables reada afore tha geh bache from tha funeral.

Blaize P'an tha Count first.

Stacia Don' know if ah should seein' as tha day as is in ud.

Blaize G'wan ghirl. Portia loved tha singin'! G'wan ud's there loochin' ah ya.

Stacia If anawan axes ud was you med me arrigh'!

Voice of McCormack comes over, Blaize listens enraptured, croons along with him.

Blaize An't he magnificent, born ony up tha road, but he goh away. There war a gramaphone an' wan rechord in our house whin ah war a ghirl. Was the Boston McGovern who brun' ud home, was a rechord a' tha Count an' ah listened ta thah rechord 'till ud was no thicher nora bubherfly's wing an me mother used to listen to ud too . . . so she used . . . yes.

Both listen to him a minute.

Turn him off now Stacia for fear tha be accusin' us of disrespec' for tha dead. Tha'll be here afore long, tomb eyed, stinchin' a' tha bone orchard. Hahe tha smell a' choffins don't you Stacia?

Stacia An't smilt enough a thim ta know Mrs Scully.

Blaize Vera partichular smell, cross atwane honeysuchle an' new mown putrefaction.

Stacia Ah wish if ya'd talche gintler abouh tha dead Mrs Scully.

Blaize Ah my age Stacia, an't natin' left ta talche gintle abouh. From here an in ud's jus' bitterness an' gums.

Stacia Portia was me friend Mrs Scully, me ony friend an' ah realize now ah didn' know her ah all. Sure ah knew she war unhappa buh who isn' these days, mus' be terrible stahe amind ta do whah she done an Maggie May toult me abouh Sly an' Marianne buh somehow thah don add up ta this . . .

Blaize Whah'd she tell ya abouh Sly an' Marianne?

Stacia Well she toult me all abouh how tha war . . .

Blaize Don' mine thah wan! Liar! Maggie May Doorley! A rusty tandem tha's all she be! Fit you behher Stacia Diyle ta mine yar own business an' noh be listenin' ta tha fabrications of a hoor.

Stacia Ah'm sorra Mrs Scully, ah didn' mane t'upseh ya.

Blaize (*calming down*) Noh upseh childt, noh upseh ah all, jus' don' pay ana attintion to thah wan.

Enter Raphael followed by Senchil, Marianne, Maggie May. All wear black, as do Stacia and Blaize.

Stacia Sih down Raphael an' lave tha hostesseries ta me.

Raphael There's drinche an' food an' all thah sourta' stuff i'tha kitchen.

Enter Maggie May from kitchen with tray of drinks. Senchil runs to help her, nearly knocks her down.

Senchil Leh me carra thah peh?

Maggie M Jay Senchil, watch where yar goin', near knocked me flah.

Blaize (*to no one in particular*) Buriet is she?

Maggie M Aye, God rest her.

Blaize (*to Raphael*) Bereft be ya? Fuchin' cheeche a'ya marryin' her i'tha first place! Who ya thinche y'are hah!

Raphael (*calls off*) Sly ya may chome in here an' tache charge a yar mother.

Blaize None a' ours ever had truche wud new money

36

afore you chem skulkin' down the valla wud natin' goin'
for ya ceptin' yar chompensation cheque in yar arse
pocket!

Raphael Ah don' nade this Mrs Scully.

Sly Mother behavin' yarself. Ah'm sorra Raphael she's a
bih upseh!

Blaize (*to Marianne*) Dry yar eyes ghirl, bin chomin' this
fifteen year. (*to Sly*) Warnt ya an' ah toult ya! Would ya
listen! (*to Maggie May*) Whiskey! Black Bush, Black label!

Maggie M Ya knows yar whiskeys Granny.

Blaize Mrs Scully ta you.

> *Silence. They all drink awkwardly, some sit, stand, lost
> in grief, exhaustion, whatever.*

Senchil Lovela Sermon.

> *Looks around, glare from Blaize. Silence from the
> others. Maggie May comes to his aid.*

Maggie M Was peh, was.

Blaize An' whah'd aither a' ye know abouh sermons,
lovela nor otherwise. (*to Maggie May*) Tha sigh' a' you in
a church'd blush tha host an' pale tha wine. Fuchin'
tinkers tha Jiyces, allas an' ever wud thar waxy blood an'
wanin' souls. Dirta igorant blood tha liches a' Belmont
never seen afore. Slainte! Ta tha Jiyces! (*Drinks.*) Ta Portia
i'tha murchy clay a' Belmont graveyard where she war
headin' from tha day she war born, cause whin ya brade
animals wud humans ya chan on'y brin' forth poor
haunted monsters who've no sinse a' God or man. Portia
an' Gabriel. Changelin's. Slainte. (*Finishes her drink,
smashes glass against wall.*) Tache me home, nex' funeral'll
be me own!

37

Sly (*to Marianne*) Be bache in a while.

Marianne Whah're ya tellin' me for.

Sly (*erupting*) You blem me for everthin'! For Gabriel an' now Portia. Ah war never hard an tha lad! Never! Leh him do whahever he wanted whin ah shoulda bin whippin' him inta shape for tha farm.

Maggie M Ah now tache ud aisy Sly.

Sly No! Lave me be! Ah druv thah childt twice a wache, ever wache ta Dublin for hees singin' lessons, in tha hay sason, whin tha chows was chalvin, whin there was more nor enough ta be done ah home. Ah druv acause you says ah should, liche a fuchen slave, seventa mile each way an' he'd sih i'tha bache a' tha char, radin' hees music booches, hummin' to heeself, wouldn' gimme tha time a' day noh if hees life depended an ud. God forgimme, buh times ah'd looche ah him through tha mirror an' tha though'd go through me mine thah this is no human childt buh some little outchaste from hell. An then he'd sing tha long drive home an' ah knew ah was listenin' ta somethin' beauhiful an' rare, though he never sang for me . . . Christ ah loved hees singin', used stan i'tha vestra a' Belmont Chapel jus ta listen ta hees practisin . . . those high notes a God he loved ta sing.

Marianne Yar greah ah feelin' long ater tha nade ta feel be ghone. This is Portia's funeral! Gabriel died fifteen year ago. Today is for Portia. Portia is dead. Portia is dead! An' you won't even mourn her.

Blaize Say somethin' Sly. Puh thah upstart in her place wance an' for all!

Raphael Will somewan geh thah woman ouha me house.

Maggie M Ah will. (*Begins wheeling Blaize backwards out of earshot of the others.*) Wan a' these days ah'm

gointa climb i'tha winda an' burn ya in yar bed . . .
(*whisper*) an' another thing, did ah ever tell ya abouh tha
time ah gev yar husban a quiche wan down Mohia Lane.

Blaize (*a hiss*) Liar, ah don believe ya!

Maggie M Oh yes ya do, acause you know an' ah know
wha's realla goin' on here, you know an' ah know whin
tha roh began an' how tha roh began.

Blaize Don' know whah yar talchin' abouh! Hoor ya.

Maggie M Ah did aye, gev him a job down Mohia Lane,
tha dirta aul' dog. Ped me wud yar egg mona, fifta quid,
an' d'ya know whah he said abouh you.

Blaize He said natin'! Yar machin' ud up.

Maggie M He says ya war a bihher aul' hag an' he'd
rather hump a bag a' rats an a bed a' nittles.

Blaize Oh listen ta tha filth a' tha hoor wud tha brochen
bottle! We war vera happa ah'll have you know.

Maggie M Happa, war yas, happa! Then ha chome he bet
tha lard a' ya evertime he lookt ah ya . . . ha chome
waches an' waches'd go by an' nowan'd have seen Blaize
Scully ouh an' abouh acause her face war in a pulp agin,
ha chome he kicked ya down tha road wance in front a
everwan . . .

Blaize Sly tache me home! Sly!

Sly begins to wheel her off, distraught.

Senchil (*eating a biscuit out of his pocket*) Whah war ya
sayin' ta her peh?

Stacia, with sandwiches for Raphael.

Stacia G'wan Raphael ate somethin.

Raphael Tha kids?

Stacia They're gran', over in my house, me sister's loochin' ater thim.

Raphael Quintin?

Stacia He's gran' . . . gran'.

They eat, drink, in silence, sound of Gabriel's voice comes over. Lights down.

Act Three

SCENE ONE

Lights up on Portia Coughlan's living room. It is set as it was at the end of Act One. Portia dozes on couch, wearing the clothes she wore at the end of Act One. It is the morning after her thirtieth birthday. We hear the sound of Gabriel Scully's voice. Portia wakes to this. It grows fainter, she strains to hear it. It stops. Portia, half sitting, half lying, lights a cigarette.

Enter Raphael Coughlan, fresh suit. He limps across the room to collect his account books, looks at Portia, she meets his look, then turns away. He goes to open curtains.

Portia Lave thim.

He does.

Raphael Ya goin' ta get tha kids reada for school or ya want me ta?

Portia You do . . . please.

Raphael looks at his watch. Stands there.

Raphael Portia.

Portia Whah?

Raphael Ah'd be willin' ta forgeh whah ya said las' nigh' if'n y'ad on'y tache ud bache.

Portia . . . D'ya want dinner this evenin'?

Raphael Whah?

Portia Dinner?

Raphael Dinner . . . yeah.

41

Portia Whah d'ya want?

Raphael For dinner?

Portia Yeah.

Raphael Anathin' ah suppose.

Portia Arrigh'.

Raphael Righ' so. (*He still stands there.*) Ya wanta come inta tha factora for a few hours?

Portia Naw.

Raphael Be good, get ya ouha tha house . . . or somethin.

Portia Can't abide tha place Raphael, ya know.

Raphael Ah . . . (*Stands there looking at her.*) Well is there anathin' ah chan do Portia? . . . Anathin'?

Portia Ah'm gran' hones'.

Raphael Quintin wants ya ta dress him for school.

Portia Will ya jus' stop! Lame me alone! Toult ya ah chan't! Arrigh'! Ah'm afraid a' thim Raphael! Whah ah may do ta thim! Don'nen ya understan'! Jaysus! Ya thinche ah don wish ah chould be a natural mother mindin' me childern, playin' wud thim, doin' all tha things a mother is asposed ta do. Whin ah looche at my sons Raphael ah sees knives an' accidents an' terrible muhilations. Their toys is weapons for me ta hurt thim wud, givin' thim a bath is a place where ah chould drown thim. An' ah have ta run from thim an lock meself away from them for fear ah cause these awful things ta happen. Quintin is safest whin ah'm nowhere near him, so teach him ta stop whingin' for me for fear ah dash hees head agin a wall or fling him through a winda.

Raphael Portia yar noh well.

Portia Ah'm arrigh' an' stop loochin' ah me as if ah'm gointa murder yees all in yeer beds, for ah won't as long as ye lave me in peace.

Raphael Ud's noh normal, tha way you're talchin' an' thinchin', noh normal ah all.

Portia Looche, if ah war goin' ta do somethin' dreadful dya think ah'd be tellin' ya bouh ud. Naw, ah'd jus' go an' do ud. Tha fac' ah'm even talchin' abouh ud manes ah wont.

Raphael An' whah sourta logic is thah?

Portia Me own, th'on'y logic ah know.

Raphael Ya stayin' home all day?

Portia Ah may.

Raphael Will ah ring Stacia ta collec' tha kids from school?

Portia Whahever.

Raphael Portia?

Portia Whah?

Raphael Ya got me scared now, ya wouldn't do anathin' ta thim, would ya?

Portia Toult ya ah wouldn't, an' ah haven't, noh a marche an thim an' ah never will . . . ah jus' want thim noh ta want anathin' from me, tha's all.

Raphael Arrigh' so . . . try an geh some slape . . . see ya this avenin'.

Portia Yeah.

Exit Raphael.

*Sound of Gabriel Scully singing. Portia registers this, runs
from the living room. Gabriel Scully appears by the bank
of the Belmont River. Disappears as Portia arrives, out of
breath. Sound of singing fades. She looks around. Silence
except for the flowing river and birdsong. Damus Halion
stands there watching her, unobserved.*

Portia Chan't ya lave me alone or present yarself afore
me! Is heaven not sa lovela ater all? Are ud's streets noh
paved in alabaster an' gold? Do th'angels not sih drinchin'
coffee an' prunin' their wings along th'eternal boulevards
a' paradise? D'ya miss me ah all?

Damus Talchin' ta tha dead now Coughlan?

Portia (*registers him*) An' whah if ah am.

Damus Some do say he still walches.

Portia Tha do say righ' . . . who toult ya anaway?

Damus Still nights he chan be heard singin' in hees high
ghirly vice. Aul Mahon swears he heard him, an' he
chomin' home ater a night's poachin ' up an O'Connor
Morriss' belt a' tha river.

Portia Ah aul Mahon, accordin' ta him everwan who ever
died walches.

Damus (*puts an arm around her*) Well ah'm alive an' dyin'
for ya me prehhy little ghos' fancier, an' though ah chan
noh haunt ya as ghosts chan, ah chan lave me marche an
ya well enough.

Kisses her. She neither resists nor complies.

If'n ya spint less time thinchin' abouh thah silla little
brother a' yours an' more time an how ah chould plase ya,
ya'd be a happa woman.

Portia (*shrugs him off*) Ah'm past all pleasures a' tha body Damus. Long past.

Damus A'ya now.

Portia An' if ya realla chare ta know, ah've allas found sex ta be a greah leh down, all thah suchin' an sweatin' an stichin' things inta wan another maches sinse ta me namore. Gimme a jigsaw or a good opera ana day or tha Belmont River. Ah'd liefer sit be tha Belmont River for five sechonds than have you or ana other man aside a' me in bed.

Damus Strong sintimints from a little cock taser who used ta geh her jiys an' thrills from watchin' min drool as she churved by, an' who, aven as she professes ta have found sex ta be a greah lehdown, is lanin' up agin me an' a flame crapin' up her throah all tha way from the bachestairs of her hot little arse.

Portia moves away from him. Looks into the river, pulls tufts of grass, flings them into the water, watches their journey.

Sulchin' now are we.

Portia Ah didn't chome here ta see you Damus Halion. Ah chem here acause this here's me father's land. This be our part a' Belmont River. So g'wan off wud yarself an' yar crude radin' a' tha world an' ud's inhabitants.

Damus Ah Portia c'man don be gettin' thiche o'er natin'.

Portia Tha discos an' hotels is full a' youn' wans who'd be on'y too glad ta have ya maulin' thim. Lave me be. Ah won't see y'agin, so there's no pint in chomin' here anamore.

Damus Portia ah bin chomin ' here on an' off this sixteen year.

Portia Ah know ha long ya bin chomin'.

Damus Don thah count for anathin? Wance ud was me ya wanted an' no wan else, or have ya forgotton thah, have ya?

Portia Ya war never more nor a distraction Damus Halion.

Damus Ah don't believe ya.

Portia Believe whah ya liche, s'tha truh.

Damus An' who's to say buh wan a' your young lads isn' mine. Ah've a mind to go an see thah cuckold a yours an tell him hees sons is noh hees sons buh mebbe mine.

Portia Thim's all Raphael's, God help them, ah med sure a' thah.

Damus Looche Portia, tha las' thin' ah want ta do is mache your life more difficult than ud is. All ah want is ta be wud ya. Why'd'n ya lave him liche ya used to say ya'd do.

Portia Used ah say ah'd lave him?

Damus Aye.

Portia Where did ah think ah was goin' . . . anaway ud maches no differ ta me whether ah'm wud you or Raphael.

Damus Ah wish ta God ah'd never led eyes an ya! Ah've puh up wud your messin' for too long now, yar runnin' bacheards an' forrards atwane me an' Raphael an' yar twin, ah'm siche a'ya Coughlan an' don't you chome loochin' for me whin yar mood changes agin for ah'll not be there for ya. Fuchen bitch, tha's all y'are an ever war.

SCENE THREE

Portia sits by the bank of the Belmont River. Maggie May's voice can be heard.

Maggie M (*off*) Portia.

Portia Over here.

Maggie M (*sees Damus departing*) Halion righ'.

Portia Righ'.

Maggie M (*sitting down beside her*) Ah'm nowan ta chaste aspersions an extra-marital dalliances buh ya chould do behher nor him. Raphael know abouh this?

Portia Raphael. On'y thing Raphael knows be how ta mache mona an' thin how ta save ud, sem as Daddy.

Maggie M Ah see. Cigareh?

Portia takes one, lies back and smokes.

Me an' me father used chome nigh' fishin' here.

Portia Used yees.

Maggie M Caugh' a piche here wance, bigger than a yennin' ewe.

Portia Mimber tha time . . .

Maggie M Whah?

Portia Ah natin' . . . thinchin' aloud is all.

Maggie M G'wan tell me.

Portia Jus' thinchin' abouh tha time tha cemetra gates fell an Gabriel.

Maggie M Aye, everwan though' he was a goner.

Portia Ah thinche ud was a sign . . . he was never righ' ater thah.

Maggie M No he wasn.

Portia What ya thinche ud meant Maggie May? Is our

47

lives followin' a minuhe an' careful plan designed an high or are we jus' flittin' from chance ta chance?

Maggie M Well there be some as says ud's impossible for a body ta be other than th'are, buh then there's others as would claim thah ya choose yar own life an' yar own machin' of ud. Personalla ah prefers ta believe thah everthin' ah've done is planned be somewan else down ta tha las' detail. Ah'm a fah aul' hoor wud bad legs Portia an' ah'd hate ta have ta lay tha blem of everthin' an meself.

Portia Whin ah war a childt Mother an' Daddy used brandish you as a threah. For years ah though' tha worst as chould ever happen me was t'en up liche you. Now ah wish ah chould.

Maggie M Liche me peh, sure ah've natin' goin' for me ceptin' Senchil. Did ah ever tell you how ah chem ta meeh him?

Portia Naw.

Maggie M People's allas laughed ah him, thinches he's an eegit, mebbe he is. See ah war in London worchin' Khing's Cross, big angra fuchers wud too much mona an' no respec'. Had this rough chustomer wan nigh', lug an him liche a scalded baboon, showed me hees fists, done hees job, tachen me mona an' shoes so as ah couldn' folly him. Ah'm lyin' there in tha duurway of an aul' warehouse, falin' a little sorry for meself, an' along chomes Senchil. He's a nigh' watchman. He taches me inta hees huh, maches me tae, turns ouh he war brough' up noh twinty mile from Belmont Valla. We talche all nigh' an' i'tha mornin' he buys me a pair a' shoon. T'war tha shoon thah done ud.

Portia Allas liched Senchil, though he's fierce fernichity.

Maggie M Senchil wasn born, he war knihhed an a weh

48

Sunda aternoon, fale safe whin he's around acause he's so fuchin' borin' natin' ever happens.

Portia Suppose he's noh there whin ah go.

Maggie M Go where, who? Whah're ya talchin' abouh peh?

Portia Afore ah was allas sure, was tha wan thing as kep' me goin' . . . now ah don' know anamore, an' yeh ah know thah somewhere he lives an' tha's tha place ah want ta be.

Maggie M An where's thah Portia?

Portia There's a wolf tooth growin' in me heart an ud's turnin' me from everwan an everthin ah am, ah wishin if tha wind or somethin' would carry me from this place athout me havin ta do anythin'.

Maggie M Peh don be talchin liche thah, gimme tha shivers.

Portia Ah knew he was goin ta do ud, planned ta do ud tagether, ah tha las minuhe ah goh afraid an he jus wint an in an' ah challed him bache buh he didn hear me an account a tha swell an' jus kep an wadın' an' ah'm standin' an tha banche, righ here, shoutin' ah him ta chome bache an' ah tha las sechond he turns thinchin' ah'm ahind him, he's face Maggie May, tha looche an hees face an' he tries ta mache tha banche buh th'undertow do have him an' a wave washes over him . . .

Maggie M Jay peh, d'ya tell yar mother an' father about this?

Portia They don liche ta talche abouh Gabriel.

Maggie M Do tha noh.

Portia Nowan does. Don know if anawan knows whah ud's liche ta be a twin. Everthin's swapped an' mixed up

49

an' yar aither two people or yar nowan. He used call me Gabriel an' ah used chall him Portia. Times we goh so confused we couldn' tell who was who an' we'd have ta wait for somewan else ta identify us an' puh us bache inta ourselves. Ah chould mache him cry be jus challin' him Portia. We didn' really liche wan another thah much whin ud chem down to ud. Oh how chan everwan be alive an' noh him? If ah chould jus see him, jus wance, ah'd be allrigh, know ah would.

Maggie M Buh tha's noh possible peh.

Pause – long pause.

Portia Ah've ta collec tha kids from school. (*Begins walking.*) Ya chomin?

Maggie M Aye.

Both exit.

SCENE FOUR

The High Chaperal. Fintan Goolan cleans a table. Enter Stacia followed by Portia with a bag of groceries. Fairly dishevelled by now.

Fintan (*cool*) Ladies.

Stacia Bottle a' cider, Portia?

Portia Natin'.

Stacia goes over to jukebox, puts on music.

Fintan (*attempting to flirt*) Overdone ud an tha whiskey las' nigh'.

Portia Ah never drinche whiskey, Fintan Goolan.

Fintan Ya war drinchin' ud las' nigh'.

Portia Drinchin' wud you don' count . . . (*Examines him*.) acause you're tha sourta man as cancels yarself ouh as soon as y'appear, th'eye fails ta register ya (*wearily*) . . . you're tha kinda cowbiy as gets shoh i'tha first scene of a bad western.

Fintan D'ya know whah you nade, Portia Coughlan?

Portia Whah do ah nade?

Fintan Ya nade tha tongue ripped ouha, an' th'arse flayed offa ya.

Portia D'ya know whah we boh nade?

Fintan Natin' you've t'offer anaway.

Portia Jus geh Stacia her drinche!

Fintan Oh, ya chan buy everthin' ceptin' good manners.

Portia A loh you'd know abouh good manners.

Fintan Bog trash is all y'are Coughlan, trumped up bog trash.

Stacia begins jiving expertly.

Stacia C'man Portia.

Portia joins her, the pair of them jive expertly, madly. Fintan comes with drink for Stacia, stands there thick as a bull.

Fintan Wan nintey! (*Price of drink.*)

Stacia Lave ud an tha table.

Portia Brandy an' ginger.

Fintan Changed yar mind.

Portia Aye.

Enter Maggie May and Senchil.

51

Maggie M Seen yar char outside, says ah'll jine ya for tha wan.

Senchil Jus tha wan.

Maggie May looks at him.

Maggie M Portia peh, glad to see y'enjiyin' yarself aven if ud is on'y two a' clache i'tha day.

Portia Come an' dance wud us.

Stacia You too Senchil.

Senchil puts his hand on his heart for reply. Maggie May takes off her shoes and joins them.

Senchil (*to Fintan*) A poh a tae, tae bag . . .

Fintan Ah know, ah know. Poh a tae, tae bag an tha side, kittle jus' off tha bile an' a brandy an' ginger for himself. (*Points to Maggie May. Goes off in a fury.*)

Senchil Yes, thanche ya. (*Proceeds to shine Maggie May's shoes which are in his keeping.*)

Portia comes over to table to drink, her mood has changed again. She stands there looking off into space holding drink, cigarette, looks upstage to river. Gabriel is there.

Arrigh' peh?

Looks at Senchil, knocks back drink, devilish glee, throws glass at Fintan who has been watching her.

Portia Sem agin! C'man Senchil. (*Takes him by the hand, they waltz.*)

Senchil Jus' for you peh.

Maggie May and Stacia sit down, drink, watch Portia and Senchil a while.

Maggie M Yar vera good ta her Stacia.

Stacia Portia allas bin good ta me . . . whin ah los' th'eye (*Touches eye-patch.*) no wan behher . . . she's noh well, Maggie May.

Maggie M Ah know.

Stacia An' her kids is in a awful stahe. Ah'm noh sayin' ud as a complaint buh they're noh minded ceptin' whah Raphael does an' they're very violent an' destructive an' ah don' know how ta tell Portia. Buh she may tache charge a' thim soon . . . mebbe ah'm worryin' too much. Portia herself war a demon of a child buh she grew up arrigh' . . . didn' she Maggie May . . . Aven if she is a bih odd.

They watch Portia and Senchil waltz a minute.

Maggie M Never knew a gintler child than Portia, liche a mouse . . . did ya know thah Marianne, Portia's mother, war a twin too.

Stacia No, never knew thah.

Maggie M There's few as does, ah'm noh aven sure Marianne knows. Marianne an' Sly is brother an' sister. Sem father, different mothers, born ithin a montha wan another.

Stacia Jay, ha chome.

Maggie M Me mother toult me an her deathbed thah Marianne was aul' Scully's childt. 'Roun' tha sem time Blaize Scully was expectin' Sly. She knows, th'oul bitch! Allas knew! Thah ah'm convinced a'.

Stacia An' she let thim marry.

Maggie M Done her bes' ta thwart ud, buh'd never own up ta tha why a' thwartin' thim. Too proud ya see; an' me mother, too ashamed, asides me father'd have kilt her if he foun' ouh, an' ah mane kilt her. Youn' Gabriel Scully war insane from too much inbreedin' an' ah'd near sweer he walched inta tha Belmont River be accident. Aither thah or hees antennae war too high, couldn' tache th'asphyxiation a' thah house.

Stacia Portia know all a' this.

Maggie M Naw, buh her blood do. Crossin' me mind these days ta tell her if ah though' ud'd do ana good, buh ah thinches ahm abouh thirta year too lahe . . . Ah don' have ta tell ya Stacia ta kape ud ta yarself.

Stacia Wont aven tell Justin an' ah tell him everthin'.

Maggie M Good ghirl.

> *Focus on Portia and Senchil dancing. Switch from song playing on jukebox to Gabriel taking up the song. Portia rests, eyes closed on Senchil, Fintan sways from side to side watching them, Maggie May and Stacia sway, drink, smoke, lost in themselves. Senchil takes a biscuit out of his pocket, nibbles on it, with his other hand he pats Portia's head lovingly. Portia looks at him.*

Portia An judgement day Senchil ya'll be atin' yar biscuits sittin' opposite a' God.

Senchil May even offer Him wan.

Portia How'd ya get ta stay so unsiled Senchil?

Senchil Unsiled, thah how ya'd ascribe me.

Portia Aye.

Senchil On'y an aul eegit Portia, whah tha world'd chall a failure.

Portia Be thah so terrible?

54

Senchil Be . . . never meh a body yeh as didn' wanta lave
a marche, some sign, however small, thah they was an tha
earth ah a pint in time. Be some as laves a good marche;
some as laves a bad wan; we shada people lave nera
marche ahall.

Portia Would ya say ah'm wan a tha shada wans?

Senchil No . . . buh even if ya war ya'd still be
necessara, a necessara bachedrop for tha giants who
walches this world an' mayhap tha nex'. (*Takes a bite of
his biscuit.*)

Stacia Portia, behher geh a move an. Kids is well ouha
school.

Fintan (*as Portia and Stacia are exiting, thick*) Sa high an'
mighy now yees don' fale ud necessara ta pay for yeer
drinches.

Portia Here!

Fintan Ah don' have change for fifty pound!

Portia Thin kape tha change. Buy yarself a new medallion.

Exit Portia and Stacia.

Maggie M Whoa. (*Grabs fifty-pound note off him.*) Ah
have change. Senchil! A fiver!

*Senchil produces a fiver in a flash. Fintan grabs it,
storms off.*
Exit Maggie May and Senchil.

SCENE FIVE

*Portia's living room. Gabriel's voice, faint, she strains to
hear it, it sounds very high up. She gets up on the table,
listens with head upward. Sits perched on the table,*

55

listening. Beside her on the table are the dishes and wine glasses from last night's dinner attempt.
    Enter Marianne Scully, looks at her.

Marianne Portia.

   No answer from Portia except an involuntary shudder.

Ah said Portia.

Portia (*eyes closed*) Ssh.

Marianne Whah i'tha name a God's wrong a' ya.

Portia Listen.

Marianne Whah?

   Looks upward.

Maggie May rang me up, says ya warn't yarself, whin is she, says I. Geh down offa thah table this minuhe youn' lady!

Portia (*looks at Marianne a while*) Ah've allas wanted ta liche ya mother buh ah never could.

Marianne Ah would ya stop such nonsense talche! Now geh down! (*gently*) Will ah help ya Portia?

   Offers a hand, Portia looks away.

Is ud Gabriel?

Portia Jus' don't! Ah don' wanta hare you talchin' abouh him, ya sully him an' me, allas.

Marianne Gabriel was fierce difficult, obsessed wud heesself an' you.

Portia Ah said not ta talche abouh him!

Marianne Well ah am an' he war obsessed wud ya! Chem ouha tha womb clutchin' yar leg an' he's still clutchin' ud

56

from wherever he is. Portia yar gointa have ta cop anta yarself. Yar home is a mess, yar childern is motherless. Raphael has ta do ud all.

Portia looks at Marianne, a look of complete and utter hatred.

An' stop loochin' ah me liche thah! If ah didn' know ya for me own dauher ah'd swear ya war some evil goblin perched up there glowerin' ah me.

Portia leaps, a wildcat leap from the table onto her mother, knocks her down, on top of her.

Me bache! Have ya lost tha run a' yarself!

Portia *(flailing at Marianne who is pinned under her)* Y'ave me suffocahed so ah chan't brathe anamore!

Marianne Lemme up! Lemme up! Portia plase, yar mother!

Portia Why chouldn' ya a' jus' lavin' us in pace! We warn doin' natin'!

Marianne Yar noh righ' i'tha head! Lemme up!

Portia Allas spyin an us!

Roars from Marianne.

Interferin' wud our games! Ouh challin' us in yar disgustin' hysterical vice! Why couldn' ya a' jus' lavin' us alone? Why?

Marianne Lave yees alone, ta yeer unnatural ways an' stupid carry on!

Portia We warn't hurtin' anaboda an' me an' Gabriel loched in thah room . . .

Marianne Ah was loched in there too.

Portia Aye, sobbin' inta tha pilla. Tha soun, thah soun', ah thinche hell be a corridoor full a rooms liche thah wan wud thah soun' chomin' from ever'wan a' thim. An' then ya'd turn an us acause we war waker an' smaller than you, buh thah war natin' compared wud yar fable attimps ta love us. We'd sooner have yar rage anaday! Yar hysterical pichnics, wud yar bottle a' orange an' yar crisps.

Marianne Tha's righ', sneer away! Ah wish ta God ye'd never been born.

Portia We wished ud too.

Marianne An Gabriel was tha wan ah loved, never you!

Portia A awful pihy then ya meant natin' ta him!

Marianne He had all tha gifts an' you had none!

Portia He hahed you! Know whah we used chall ya! Tha stuche pig!

Marianne You war on'y hees shada trailin' ater him liche a slavish pup!

Portia Ya fuchen liar ya! Ya chome in here talchin' abouh Gabriel as if y'ownt him! He war mine first! An' ah lost him first! Ah was th'ony wan thah mahhered ta him!

Marianne Mahhered ta him! Ah seen whah he used do ta ya! How he used start ya chochin' be jus lookin ah ya! How he used draw blood from ya whin ya tried ta defy him!

Portia Mother, he war doin thim things to heeself for he thought I war him.

Marianne Ah know he did! Buh yar noh him Portia! Ya have ta forgeh him, ya chant go an liche this.

Portia Why'd ya have ta sever us?

Marianne Wasn me as severed yees an' well ya know ud!

Portia Ya fuchen bitch! Geh ouh! Geh ouh! Geh ouh!

Marianne Stop ud! Stop ud! Thah's enough a thah!

Portia Ud wasn me as severed us! Was you an Daddy! Was ye stopt hees singin' lessons!

Marianne Me an' yar father woulda stopt lohs a thin's if we coulda . . .

Portia Didn ya know th'only fuchen thing he chould do was sing!

Marianne Gabriel stopt singin' Portia whin you stopt talchin' to him, whin ya refused ta go anawhere wud him, whin ya refused to eah ah tha table wud him, whin ya ran from ever room he walched inta, whin ya started runnin' round wud Stacia an' Damus Halion. Thah's whin Gabriel stopt singin'. Oh Portia ya done away wud him as if he war na more nor a ear a chorn ah tha threshin' an' me an' yar father chould do natin' an'y looche on.

Enter Sly unobserved, with package.

Portia Mother stop, ah chan't bear ud . . . Christ I love this world, tha colours of ud an' I wanta be in ud steada this dying thing flowin' through me, this forever dying thing as jus wants me ta cuurse tha waves liche an aul glob a jetsam. Mother, tha nigh he died, tha nigh after our fifteenth birtha, ah walkt down ta tha river wud him an' he whispered ta me afore he wint in. 'Portia', he says, 'ah'm goin' now buh ah'll chome bache an' ah'll kape chomin' bache till ah have ya.'

Marianne Ya war wud him Portia?

Sly (*half to himself*) Wud him.

Marianne An' ya didn stop him.

59

Portia Stop him. Wan of us was goin', war khillin' each other an' ye jus left us ta figh ud ta tha deah, well we fough ud ta tha deah an' I won. Mother I chan hare him chomin towards me, chan hare him challin' me . . .

Sly Ya war wud him, Portia how chould ya, an' ya leh him go.

Marianne Sly, lave ud.

Sly An' ya leh us search high an' low for him, hopin' agin hope we'd fine him alive, puttin' off draggin' tha river, an' ya knew where he war tha whole fuchen time. Me on'y son, an' ya leh him go liche a swalla ah tha close a summer.

Portia Ah didn plan for not ta go wud him . . . jus happened.

Sly Ya cunt! Ya darche fuchen cunt! Ah watched how you played wud him, how ya tased him, ah watched yeer perverted activihies, ah seen yees dancin' in yeer pilts, disgustin', an' tha whoile world aslape barrin' ye an' tha river . . . Ah'll sourt you ouh wance an' for all ya little hoor ya, ya rip, ya fuchen bitch ya . . .

Portia Ah'm noh yar wife nor yar mother so don you chome in her tachin' yar rage ouh an me ya fuchen coward ya!

Marianne Sly! Ga home now! Yar own dauher!

Portia (*to Sly*) Ah didn khill yar precious Gabriel. We all did!

Sly You're noh my dauher anymore.

Portia Daddy don say thah ta me, ah'm jus tryin' ta tell ya how ud was. He's closin' in an me. An' hare hees foohfall crossin' tha worlds.

60

Sly Whah ya want me ta do ghirl, ah dale wud animals noh ghosts . . . whah ya want me ta do . . . Marianne say somethin' to her . . . Ah'm noh able. (*Goes to exit, picks up package.*) An' there's tha dress ya toult me ta collec from town for her birtha. (*Exiting, turns to look at Portia, hold.*)

Marianne (*gently*) G'wan Sly, g'wan.

And exit Sly. Silence. Marianne opens package, takes out a beautiful dress, holds it against Portia.

D'ya liche ud?

Portia (*a whisper*) Mother.

Marianne Ud'll be beauhiful an ya . . . wanted ta have ud for yesterda . . . For yar thirtieth birtha. (*And exit Marianne.*)

SCENE SIX

Portia sets the table, lights candles, opens wine, pours a glass, drinks. Sits, passage of time. Puts on diamond bracelet. Enter Raphael. Phone, car keys, factory book, looks at table with pleasure.

Raphael Kids in bed?

Portia Jus gone.

Raphael Goh held up ah the factora.

Portia Did ya. (*Pours him a glass of wine.*)

Raphael Thanks . . . falin' behher?

Portia Fale jus' fine.

Raphael Glad ta hare ud.

Portia Ah'll brin' in tha dinner if yar reada.

Raphael Belt away.

Portia brings in the dinner, serves it up. They dig in, eat like peasants, heads close to the plate, no conversation, horse down the dinner, finished.

Portia There's more.

Raphael Gran' for tha minuhe.

Raphael lights a cigar, Portia a cigarette.

Ah wint ta see tha barman a' tha High Chaperal . . . Goolan, thah hees name?

Portia Fintan Goolan, aye.

Raphael Sweers he never led a finger an ya.

Portia Aye.

Raphael Is ud true . . . Ud is isna . . . Portia why'd ya lie abouh somethin' liche thah?

Portia Mayhap ta hide a bigger wan.

Raphael Whah ya mane?

Portia Channen we jus lave ud Raphael! Looche! Ah chooked yar dinner. Ah poured yar wine, ah bahed Quintin, read him a story an' all. Chant we knoche a bih a pleasure ouha wan another for wance?

Raphael Pleasure? Tha pair of us? Tha mind boggles, Portia . . . Anaway, long realized ya want vera little ta do wud me.

Portia May have wanted more ta do wud ya if ya warn't allas sa chalm an' unnady Raphael . . . never learnt how ta dale wud thah . . . An ah never toult anawan this afore . . . ya see, me an' Gabriel med love all tha time, down be

62

tha Belmont River amon tha swale . . . from th'age a' five
. . . thah's as far bache as ah chan amimber anaways . . .
buh ah thinche we war doin' ud afore we war born. Times
ah close me eyes an' ah fale a rush a' waher 'roun' me, an'
above we hear tha thumpin' a' me mother's heart, an'
we're atwined, hees fooh an me head, mine an hees foetal
arm, an' we don' know which of us be th'other an' we
don't wanta, an' tha waher swells 'roun' our ears an' all
tha world be Portia an' Gabriel packed forever in a tigh'
hoh womb, where there's no brathin', no thinchin', no
seein', on'y darcheness an' heart drums an' touch . . . An'
whin ah war fifteen ah slep' wud Damus Halion . . .
Shoulda knowed behher, he meant natin' ta me . . . an'
Gabriel seen an Gabriel seen an' never spoche ta me ater.

Raphael Ud's me yar married ta Portia, noh Gabriel an
ud's me ya bin fuchen round an, noh Gabriel. Damus
Halion. Jaysus. Portia, yar so much behher than him!
Why'd ya lower yarself an me wud him?

Portia Toult ya he meant natin' ta me Raphael, natin'.

Raphael An' I don chare abouh Damus Halion anymore,
though' I did, he's on'y a fuchen eegih of a gobshite father.
Gabriel's tha wan. Ah've waihed thirteen year for you ta
talche abouh me tha way ya've jus tached abouh him.
(*Gets up to exit.*) Ah'm weary of ud all.

Portia Raphael don lave me here be me own.

Raphael Don know whah way ah'm asposed ta behave
wud ya anymore. Ya thinche ya chan do whah ya liche
wud me. Wance ya chould. Whin I first seen you walchin'
be tha river ah prayed ta God ta leh me have ya, ah
showered ya hud everthin' ah though' a woman chould
want an' whah do you do? (*Pause.*) Ya've savaged me ta
tha scuh an' now ya want love talche, well ah've none for
ya. Ah'm goin ta bed.

Portia Raphael.

Raphael Looche we'll talche abouh ud tomorra, ah'm tired Portia.

Portia Raphael.

Raphael Whah?

Portia I seen you long afore you ever seen me.

Raphael Whah?

Portia Seen ya fishin' wan Sunda afternoon an' tha stillness an' sureness thah chem offa ya was a balm ta me, an' whin I axed who ya war an' tha said thah's Raphael Coughlan, 'Raphael' ah though'. How chan somewan wud a name liche thah be so rale, an' ah says ta meself if Raphael Couglan nohices me ah will have a chance t'inter the world an stay in tha world which has allas bin tha battle for me. An' you say ya want me ta talche abouh you tha way ah talche abouh Gabriel? Ah cannoh Raphael, ah cannoh, an' though everwan an everthin' tells me ah have ta forgeh him, ah cannoh Raphael, ah cannoh.

Exit Raphael.

(*a whisper*) Come an little brother, come an, show me wance more tha fah river dark of yar heart.

Gabriel's voice comes over, triumphant.
Lights down.